THE JOBLESS ECONOMY?

To Harold and Margaret, my parents,
Christopher and Robert, my sons,
and all my relations and friends who
have given me help and encouragement.

The Jobless Economy?

Computer Technology in the World of Work

Michael Dunkerley

Polity Press

The right of Michael Dunkerley to be identified as author of this work has been asserted in accordance with the Copyright, Designs and Patents Act 1988.

First published in 1996 by Polity Press in association with Blackwell Publishers Ltd.

2 4 6 8 9 10 7 5 3 1

Editorial office:
Polity Press
65 Bridge Street
Cambridge CB2 1UR, UK

Marketing and production:
Blackwell Publishers Ltd
108 Cowley Road
Oxford OX4 1JF, UK

Published in the USA by
Blackwell Publishers Inc.
238 Main Street
Cambridge, MA 02142, USA

ISBN 0-7456-1577-5
ISBN 0-7456-1578-3 (pbk)

A CIP catalogue record for this book is available from the British Library and the Library of Congress.

Typeset in 10 on 12 pt Garamond
by Graphicraft Typesetters Ltd, Hong Kong
Printed in Great Britain by T.J. Press, Padstow, Cornwall

This book is printed on acid-free paper.

Contents

Acknowledgements

The author and publishers would like to thank the following for permission to use copyright material:

Business Week for the use of Figure 6.2 on p. 69; The *Calgary Sun* for the extract of the article on p. 68; The Central Statistical Office and the Controller of HMSO for the use of Table 7.1 (from *Business Monitor* PA 1003 1993), Crown copyright 1993; Zvi Griliches and *Quarterly Journal of Economics* for Figure 8.2 (© 1994 by the President and Fellows of Harvard College and the Massachusetts Institute of Technology); Dow Jones & Co Inc. for extracts from an article in *Barrons*, 'Is a Superfluous Population becoming an American Fixture?' 1994, reproduced by permission of *Barrons*, © Dow Jones & Co. Inc, all rights reserved worldwide; The Economist Books Ltd for two figures from *Pocket World in Figures* (Hamish Hamilton/the Economist 1994), © The Economist Books; The Economist Newspapers Ltd for four figures from *Pocket Britain in Figures* (Hamish Hamilton/The Economist 1995), © The Economist Newspapers Ltd; *Financial Times* for extracts from two articles (pp. 6 and 112); The Institute of Management for an extract from the Institute of Management's Long Term Employment Strategies (1994) (p. 91); *Management Today* for Figure 4.1; Mirror Syndication International for the extract from an article from the *Sunday Mirror* (p. 59) © *Daily Mirror*; Isabel V. Sawhill for Table 1.1 (from Isabel V. Sawhill, ed., *Challenge to Leadership: Economic and Social Issues for the Next Decade* (The Urban Institute Press, Washington DC 1988) as reprinted in *The Politics of Rich and Poor* by Kevin Philips); Southam Editorial Services for an extract from an article by Julian Beltrame in the *Vancouver Sun,* (8 August 1995).

Every effort has been made to trace all copyright holders. However, if any have been inadvertently overlooked, the publishers will be pleased to make the necessary arrangements at the first opportunity.

Introduction

This book has been written largely from personal observation and experience. I have had three careers to date and may well have one or two more before I retire. I don't regret the way things are working out and I enjoy the variety, but there is a downside in that there is less security and there is less certainty as to salary and pension levels. This is the brave new world we are in and my book sets out to explain why economic events are taking the direction that they are.

Within two years of leaving university I established my own company in the food industry which prospered for fourteen years. I then became involved in commercial property development and management for a time. In 1988, at the age of forty one, I started out on a new career selling software to industrial companies. This has provided another fascinating insight into commercial life, but in particular it has revealed for me the true extent of technological revolution that is taking place. Over the last seven years I have talked to hundreds of people who are being affected by technology and visited scores of factories that are being re-organized because of new technology. This covers nationally based companies and multi-national corporations. The situations that I describe in the chapters that follow are nearly all from first-hand experience. I am both excited by and afraid of the potential that new technology has.

Why should any company invest £100,000, £500,000 or £1 million and more in installing computers and sophisticated software? They do it because it is a more efficient way of doing business. What are the ways of doing business that are being replaced? Almost without exception they involve employing people.

A special language has developed to sugar the pill when the impact of new technology is being discussed. Companies 'downsize' or 'right size', people are 'let go' or 'released', the 'fat is trimmed' and the new organization becomes 'lean and mean' ready to take on 'world class' competition and win. We all clap and cheer these positive images until we too become victims. Of course, the competition has also been doing the same thing, so in order to stay ahead, companies have to revisit the fountainhead of new technology for their next fix and so it goes on.

New technology can mean new products and services. That is all for the good. However it can also mean replacing people with cheaper and more efficient machines which has more dubious value. As our understanding of efficiency gained through this route matures we come full circle so that new products and services too are introduced to the market with the minimum of costly human involvement. What many have yet to realize is that without people, and well paid people, there will be no new markets. However, that problem lies beyond the next election or the next set of annual accounts.

New technology will find its way into the hands of rich and powerful organizations and individuals. They will use it to suit their own agendas. The majority of the world's people are neither rich nor powerful, but they must make sure that their interests too are served by our new technology because it can be used to enrich everyone's lives. The solutions that I propose are simple. However, they will strike at the roots of many people's belief systems.

It used to be possible to say 'It won't happen for a long time yet'. It is no longer possible to say that any more.

1

Are We on a Fool's Journey?

One evening an office colleague said to me 'Where has all the leisure time gone?' It was a pleasant, sunny, late spring evening. The time was half past seven and we were still at work even though a normal eight-hour day would have officially ended two hours previously.

That chance remark set me thinking and started the process going that has led to the writing of this book. Working late for us was not untypical. Other colleagues were there too and some would still be there hours later. We were not compelled to do the extra work, we did it voluntarily. The company we worked for paid well, but it operated in a competitive environment and there were often tight deadlines to meet. If we wanted to win the business and to keep it then we had to let the customers' deadlines rule our lives from time to time.

Away from the office other colleagues who had done a full day's work at customer sites would be driving back home with the prospect of not arriving there until well after their children had gone to bed. Their view of that pleasant evening would be through a car windscreen on a busy motorway.

We probably had it easier than many others. In the highly competitive world of the big company excessively long hours seem to be the order of the day. Surveys of American business executives show that on average they work fifty-four hours a week and only take two weeks holiday a year. That is an average working day of eleven hours. Take out eight hours for sleep and make an allowance for travelling to and from work and it is obvious that there is little room in their lives for anything else other than work. However, these people, willingly or unwillingly, are part of the minority of the population who define their identity predominantly in terms of their work. André Gorz quotes research in Germany that suggests that maybe no more than 15 per cent of the overall population see themselves in this way. The figure rises, as might be expected, to 35 per cent amongst managers.[1]

Being busy and active is better than having nothing to do. For a time this type of high pressure activity and the money that goes with it can even be fun until, that is, the novelty wears off. Then thoughts about the quality of life eventually catch us up and force us to question why and for what purpose we are behaving in this way. We probably hope to get lucky and make enough money to be able to opt out but the reality is that if we want our families to have the good life then this is a life sentence. The hassle and the pressure are not going to go away. It could even get worse as international competition becomes fiercer.

However, whilst some of us have all the work and are short of leisure there are millions of other people who have all the leisure and none of the work. Their leisure is enforced and without the benefit of the money with which to enjoy it. They are skilled people who could do the work. They are able people who would love the chance to become skilled and join in. Are we letting them down and at the same time blighting our own lives? It is certainly possible to share the work with them but the real challenge is to do so without suffering pay cuts or seeing our living standards fall. This is after all what has been happening in the recent past. Again recent German experience demonstrates that between 1960 and 1990 productivity trebled whilst annual working hours fell 25 per cent from 2,150 hours to 1,650 hours. Even before this, weekly working hours in general throughout the industrialized world have fallen from around 65 hours at the start of the century to around the 40 hours we experience today. This has happened as the worst abuses of the industrial revolution have been eliminated and ordinary working people have started to enjoy the benefits of the more affluent society their labours have created. It should therefore be possible to continue this trend into the future, if we have the political and social will to do so.

What my friend was referring to when he asked the question 'Where has all the leisure time gone?' was the promise, widely believed in the 1960s, that science and technology would bring leisure and prosperity to the world. The mood of the 1960s was optimistic and adventurous. My children, who are at college now, laugh at the funny fashions we used to wear and the old photographs are amusing. But the photographs can't speak and tell them that we had very high hopes for the future and that those hopes have not been fulfilled. The students of today are more cynical about their chances than we ever were. We put our faith in science and technology. After all, if President John Kennedy could command the American scientists to put a man on the moon within the decade and his successors actually saw it happen on time, then nothing could be beyond us once we put our collective, scientific will to the task.

I can remember wondering if the age for retirement would be reduced to fifty years and if so how we would all spend our leisure time after then? Alternatively we might work for longer but have to do only a three-day week. Commentators speculated about how the new machines and technologies were going to free us from drudgery and banish forever starvation and poverty. That was thirty years ago. Today the younger generations are wondering if science and technology will prevent them from ever getting a job and many older people know that it has already done them out of their jobs.

Instead of being a golden age, the early 1990s witnessed one of the most severe economic depressions ever. Unemployment rose to new highs, families had their homes repossessed, a record number of children were raised in poverty and pensioners were told that in future the state might not be able to afford their pensions. Some say our present standards of living are too high and that we should expect to see them fall gradually over the next twenty years. And yet the science and technology at our command have become better, more clever and more reliable. In fact the cleverer and more reliable they become the worse things seem to be getting. What is going wrong?

The situation of that summer evening was made more ironic for me by the fact that I and my colleague were both working in the computer industry. Computers are supposed to free society from mental drudgery – and they do, but in the process they inevitably do away with jobs. Ideally people thus helped out of drudgery are expected to be able to find more rewarding employment elsewhere. The reverse is proving to be true. Many of the people made redundant by automation are only able to find new jobs at very low levels of pay or as part-time workers. The ultimate irony is the fact that the computer industry itself, so long a major employer paying high wages, is now one of the chief beneficiaries of its own efficiencies. Job losses in companies making computer hardware are running at tens of thousands a year. Everywhere highly skilled and intelligent people are being told that their skills are now obsolete. Skills that are less than twenty years old are now being superseded by new skills whose life span can only be guessed at but which at best will last a shorter time than those they are replacing. In fact the technology is changing so quickly that an interview in *Computer Weekly* reports that the useful life of most IT skills is down to three years with obsolescence following within six years. To rub salt into the wounds the article also reports that employers are not always willing to fund the training necessary to keep staff up-to-date and that staff are increasingly having to pay for it themselves.[2]

Once again, what has gone wrong and why has the promise of a better world receded like a mirage? Few of us are Luddites. We mostly want the new technology. We tend to like using it and can see the real benefits that it brings. What is wrong with such a future? What is wrong with machines and computers doing the work for the people? In one hundred years' time, in the closing years of the next century, do we really expect our great-great-grandchildren to be working eight hours a day, five days a week for forty or fifty years of their lives at jobs they tolerate or even hate? The answer is surely no.

The 2090s may seem a long way away, especially to western business leaders who are trained to think no further than the next three months' profit figures. However, other cultures see things in longer time scales. They think in terms of generations and have concern for the type of world that they will pass down to their grandchildren. I knew all my grandparents. They were born in the 1890s. I will live to know my grandchildren and they will live to see the 2090s. There are five generations, but they overlap and the link from the nineteenth century to the twenty-first century and maybe the twenty-second century is made by just three individuals. My grandparents witnessed the worst of the industrial revolution. I want my grandchildren to witness the best.

There is an idea doing the rounds in some influential circles that living standards should be flexible and go down, as well as up, to reflect the interplay of economic forces. The next generation may have to accept lower living standards than we have experienced. It may come as a surprise that thoughts of falling living standards are being seriously considered in government think tanks and the board rooms of international corporations. A leading article in the *Financial Times* with senior business leaders discussing American international competitiveness put it this way.

> Again it comes back to the standard of living. The American tradition is based on the expectation of rising wealth. Large parts of the population are now faced with the reality of being poorer than their parents, or even their grandparents. The price of international competitiveness may thus be the lowering of expectations, not only for wages but for working hours and conditions. In the US, the lesson is proving painful. Europe, for the most part, has yet to confront it.[3]

There will be continuing scientific and technological progress and that means there will be change. The problem is that our social attitudes are not keeping up with the pace of change in our technology. If we want to enjoy the benefits that are there for the taking we are going to have to change some of our ideas; otherwise we are embarking on a fool's journey.

Conventional economic thinking assumes that people will act rationally, or nearly rationally, and that markets will work perfectly, or nearly perfectly. However, people do not always act rationally; often they act emotionally and then rationalize their choices if they need to. Is it really rational for someone who already has more money than they can spend to continue to work six days a week just to make more? Socially, the consequence is increasing economic polarization between the affluent and the poor. Some believe that this concentration of wealth and power will be mitigated by 'trickle-down' spending. Unfortunately 'trickle-down' spending by the affluent minority of the population has always been too weak a mechanism to significantly improve the lot of whole populations. It is like throwing a pebble into a lake. There is a lot of activity in the immediate vicinity of impact, but the ripples soon vanish to nothing. People only spend what money they have to, or want to, and then they hoard the rest with inevitable consequences.

Trickle-down investment used to have some impact on employment prospects, but new technology is calling that into question. Siemens, the German electronics giant, has just announced plans to build a hi-tech factory in the North-East of England to manufacture computer chips. The firm selected the location because, in their own words, the labour force was flexible, skilled and would work for relatively low wages. The total investment is put at £1 billion and the number of jobs to be created is 3,000. That is a huge investment just to create 3,000 relatively low-paid jobs. It is over £330,000 per job. At this rate it will take investment of approximately the entire GDP of the British economy for a year just to put back to work half the nation's unemployed and underemployed people.

Again, looking at America where competition and the profit motive are given the fullest expression, the winning top 4 per cent of the population earn a staggering $454 billion a year altogether. This is the same amount as the total earnings of the bottom 51 per cent of the population.[4]

The situation is getting worse. Between 1981 and 1986 the share of the Gross Domestic Product going to the wealthiest 1 per cent of the population rose from 8 per cent to 15 per cent.[5] Despite the hype of the time the decade of the 1980s and its experiment with raw market economics was a success for only a relatively few people. Table 1.1 is reproduced from *The Politics of Rich and Poor.*[6]

The trend is similar in the UK. A report from the Fiscal Studies Institute entitled *For Richer, For Poorer* puts the picture bluntly. In 1977 there were 3 million poor people in the UK or about 6 per cent of the population

Table 1.1   *Family income gains and losses 1977–1988*

Income decile	Percentage change	Dollar value of change
First	−14.8%	−$609
Second	−8.0%	−$665
Third	−6.2%	−$813
Fourth	−6.6%	−$1,216
Fifth	−6.3%	−$1,507
Sixth	−5.4%	−$1,619
Seventh	−4.3%	−$1,577
Eighth	−1.8%	−$798
Ninth	+1.0%	+$577
Tenth	+16.5%	+$16,913

Additional detail		
Top 5%	+23.4%	+$31,473
Top 1%	+49.8%	+$134,513

Source: *Challenge to Leadership*, Urban Institute

on less than half average earnings. In 1991 this figure had risen to 11 million people or about 20 per cent of the population. It includes low-paid self-employed people, low-paid full-time workers, retired people over sixty years old, unemployed people, students, disabled people, etc. From 1977 the earnings of the richest 10 per cent really took off so that they now receive 25 per cent of the national income with just 3 per cent going to the poorest 10 per cent of the population.[7]

Howard Davies, Deputy Governor of the Bank of England, put it this way.

> We can't go on like this, watching inequality grow and grow, without beginning to pay a high price for social division. Our social stability, educational traditions and national wealth should have been able to deliver more rapidly rising standards of living for the population. The fact that they have not, and that we are left with a large lump of either unemployed or very low paid people, is a drag anchor on the economy.[8]

In the 1980s capitalism may finally have defeated communism as a wealth-creating system, but it has not yet come to terms with sharing out the wealth created and the potential for leisure that could be ours as well. Could this just be the competitive, workaholic minority trying to sell the majority a suspect bill of goods or is something else going on? Has the world of science and technology moved on to the point where we must now rethink our outdated economic nostrums?

2

Looking the Gift Horse in the Mouth

The advance of science and technology is offering us a gift, but do we know how to receive it? The gift could be nothing less than prosperity for all, and not just those people who are able to grab it for themselves. Technology is not at fault, it is delivering its end of the bargain. The problem lies with us, because we are so focused by our history on the problem of the creation of wealth that we are neglecting the other side of the coin, which is the consumption of the wealth we are creating. Until now the link has been made for us. The link has been the job.

Technology is a powerful creator of jobs, until the moment it becomes mature and breaks free of human involvement. Its development cycle can be likened to that of a human being. It has an infant stage, an adolescent stage, a mature stage and an old age.

In the infant stage, technology is full of promise, but needs constant care and attention because there are so many things that it is still not able to do for itself, or that are not understood about it. This creates jobs. In its adolescent stage, it becomes more confident and adventurous and pushes itself out into new areas. This is when technology genuinely opens up new horizons for us, and creates new jobs in areas that were never before imagined. Like any teenager, it also has a tendency to scorn traditional values as it tries to reshape the world to its liking. When it brushes up against older, less suitable technology, it pushes it aside, and with it the jobs associated with that older technology. In its mature stage the technology is well understood and can fend for itself. It does not need to be supervised so heavily or explained so much. It does not require assistance to get on with its work. Jobs are eliminated but it still delivers the goods. In its old age it is subject to attack and replacement by a younger challenger.

Technology is also applied to processes. The products that we buy in shops are rarely the object of one activity. They are the sum total of a series of activities that make up a process. The first operation in the creation of a loaf of bread is to grow the wheat. The next activity is to mill the grain. The next activity is to bake the bread. The next activity is to deliver it to the shops and so on. Each of these activities has its own technology and each technology falls to the onslaught of progress at a different time. When one activity in the chain is automated, its productive potential rises, and this puts a strain on the preceding and following activities to keep up. They can only do this by applying more of the same technology that is available at each of these stages. Traditionally this has meant more people. Consequently, at these bottlenecks employment opportunities rise, as do wages. Thus, the mix of new technology and its uneven introduction into the chain of production, has the potential to raise, by a leveraged factor, both the employment potential and the earning potential of large populations. When technologies, and the whole process to which they belong, mature, the potential for causing unemployment and reduced earning power is just as great. The health of this system depends upon the introduction of new labour-intensive technologies to balance the old maturing technologies.

Each process of linked operations is itself part of a larger family of technology that is also maturing. There has been the age of water power, the age of steam power, the age of the internal combustion engine and, more recently, the age of electronics. As one has faded the next one has taken over. However, these too fit into their own overall process, namely that of industrialization. On a world scale, the whole process of industrialization has now been going on for 250 years. It has gone through the infant stage and it is nearing the end of the adolescent stage. Agriculture in advanced economies is already in its mature stage and offers minuscule employment opportunities. In 1890 the average American farm grew enough surplus food to feed five extra people. Today the average American farmer grows enough surplus food to feed ninety-five extra people. The industrial sectors are about to join it by entering their mature stage. There is always the possibility of new technology coming along to start the whole process off again, but if it does, it won't be of the same nature as that with which we are familiar. We can't unlearn the lessons of efficiency that we have learnt, and the sparing way that we now use human labour. Any new process will not be starting from the same baseline of labour-intensive technology.

There is another reason why the next cycle of economic development won't make use of people in the same way as before. One aspect of the old technology of the passing industrial revolution was that, in relation to people, the technology ultimately became expensive. It became expensive because it became bulky. The bigger something is, and the heavier something is, the more it is going to cost, because it consumes more raw materials in its manufacture, its transportation to the market place and its maintenance. The giant machines of the smokestack industries may be physically impressive, but by today's standards they are expensive and wasteful in their consumption of labour and particularly materials. Competition exerts downward pressure on the price of any technology, but the break-even point remains high for mechanical technology, for the reasons already given, limiting the extent to which it can replace the human element.

The technology coming forward today is the exact opposite. Its costs are loaded to the front end, and not the back end, as was the case with mechanical machines. The costs are in the development of the new technology more than they are in the manufacture of the product itself. Computers are a typical example of this. They cost millions of pounds to develop but they are light and compact when delivered to market. The cost of raw materials in an expensive computer is a tiny fraction of the overall cost of the product. Low-skill, low-cost labour can now be used in the assembly process. This favours low prices and low prices need volume sales to recoup the investment. A new hi-tech product may start out expensive, but as the break-even point is low on each additional unit, competition will chase the price down to lower levels, making volume sales even more essential to recover costs. The ultimate example of this is computer software. It can take teams of analysts and programmers to write a complex piece of software, and the first copy might stand the authors $10,000,000. However, each additional copy of that software costs only as much to produce as the computer tape it is copied on to, which can be as low as $10.

The dilemma is this. As progress continues, we expect to become richer and this translates into higher wages. At the same time the technology that we are now working with is becoming both smarter and cheaper. This either forces us out of jobs entirely, or forces us to lower our wages to match the costs of the new technology, which year on year is becoming cheaper. In America workers have been fired and then rehired at lower wages. In the UK the process has been more subtle. Services have been contracted out, particularly as part of the privatization process, where public services have been sold into private ownership. This means that workers have continued in the same job without a break, but with a new employer and new, less favourable, terms and conditions of employment. Even if the workers concerned have not always been competing directly with new technology, they face a labour market where numbers are swollen by people who have, and this depresses pay rates just the same. New research suggests that within a local economy, a 2 per cent increase in unemployment can reduce local pay rates by up to 10 per cent.

The average wage in the United Kingdom in 1993 was around £18,000 a year according to the Inland Revenue. The United Kingdom is not a particularly high-wage economy, and many industrial economies pay higher wages. The total costs of employing a person can be doubled, to take into account the cost of employment benefits, sick pay, pensions, office accommodation and the like. This means that the average cost of employment is around £36,000 per year per person. Over a five-year period this multiplies out to £180,000.

Most industrial machinery is written off over a period of five years. For £180,000 an impressive amount of machinery can be purchased. At the time of writing, this sum will buy two computer-controlled machine tools that will run unattended once they are set up. It will purchase three articulated trucks. It will purchase an advanced multi-user computer system, with which just a few people can control the accounting, manufacturing, stock control and distribution functions of a large company. What is more, all this technology will be cheaper next year. If any of these representative purchases can make one average wage-earner redundant, they will have paid for themselves. If they can make five people redundant then the company will save itself £1,000,000 over five years. People are now becoming the most expensive optional component of the productive process and technology is becoming the cheapest. People are now specifically targeted for replacement just as soon as the relevant technology is developed that can replace them.

A certain percentage of the population are clever enough to be able to stay ahead of the technology, and to find continuing employment at the leading edge, where wages might even be higher than before. This keeps the average pay figure high, but masks the fact that the range of pay differentials is widening. The choice for most people who are not able to work at the leading edge appears to be to take redundancy now or to take a cut in real wages each year, as the technology that they are competing with becomes incrementally cheaper. This is a very gloomy scenario, but one that is all too likely to be proved true by events unless some new, labour-intensive, high-waged technology rescues us.

However, is this the only message that can be read from the situation we find ourselves in? Could the real message be that there isn't really a problem at all, except for the one that we are making for ourselves?

Certainly people are becoming too expensive as a means of production when measured against our clever machines and they are being replaced. This is excellent news. The machines are now doing the work. We can do less. The output of goods and services is still there to be enjoyed. In that sense we are certainly no poorer as a society. We just lack the wit and wisdom to work out how to distribute the production of our increasingly automated production process, whilst we set about enjoying life more. Our economic thinking, our political thinking, and our moral thinking are firmly stuck in the competitive past. If there is no need to work at creating the basics of food, power, and other commodities, because automatic machines are doing the work, can we cope with the idea that these goods will eventually be free in the future? What need have robots for wages? It is quite a revolutionary thought to get used to, but for most people ultimately a very agreeable one.

This idea will have to be taken very seriously even though it might seem absurd at the moment. We are a consumer economy, in which the consumers get their money by being able to be a part of the process of production, by being able to work in the system. To date, no part of the economic system has been able to function without human involvement. There has been greater efficiency but, fortunately, economic growth has pulled more people into the system at enhanced wages and therefore has created more consumers to purchase the products of that growth. It has been a virtuous spiral, promising rising living standards for the majority of the population.

For the first time in our history we are looking at the widespread use of technology that will produce what we need whilst at the same time employing steadily fewer people and ultimately no people. In other words, for the first time in our history we are no longer creating consumers for that output. It does not matter that displaced workers might be finding other 'work'. In so far as that other work is low-paid, then they cease to be the consumers that they once were, and we have demand deficit. Even if they are the fortunate minority who are well paid in a new industry, then their demand will only represent the inputs and outputs of the industry that they are working in. It will not compensate for the lack of demand from the more numerous, but non-existent, workers in traditional industries that are now running on automatic. Certainly the system will adjust to these new circumstances, but it will adjust by winding down.

The owners of industries that manage to achieve 'workerless' status, particularly if they are producing something that we need, will still try to exact a price from the market. This will then take one of two directions. If they are able to establish a monopoly, or a cartel, then they will be successful. People with money will simply have to pay up. People without will have to do without. If they are not successful, then competition will drive the price down towards zero, which is much the same thing as giving the product away free. Totally automatic production lines, serviced robotically, will be external to, and independent from, the economy inhabited by humans. There will be no real costs to underpin their prices. Control of this productive capacity will cease to be an economic matter and it will become a political issue. How long before this happens? It is estimated that human knowledge doubled between 1750 and 1850. Today it is estimated that human knowledge is doubling every ten years. Given the unimaginable changes that have taken place over the last fifty years since the end of the Second World War, my guess is that it will happen in the next fifty years, by which time accumulated human knowledge, particularly scientific knowledge, will be thirty-two times greater than it is today. However, be it forty years or sixty years, it will be in the lifetime of my children.

The reaction of many people to the above statement will be 'It cannot be done' or even 'It should not be done'. Those who say it can't be done, do so after looking at history and seeing that poverty, and worse, has always been part of the human condition, and see no reason why that should ever change. Poverty, and the fear of poverty, has disciplined mankind for thousands of years, and they fear the consequences of removing this yoke. Those who say it should not be done do so after consulting their moral values, which tell them that if you don't work you don't deserve to eat, even if it is offered to you on a plate. In either case, these, or other inappropriate attitudes, preclude them from even investigating ways in which it might be done. A sort of herd instinct takes over, as everyone agrees that it is impossible and no-one wants to break ranks.

There is all manner of economic activity to confuse the picture. There is the cut and thrust of competition, national and international, fair and unfair. There are always economic cycles such as trade cycles at work, but it is the message of this book that we are all now caught up in larger cycles to do with our development and use of technology. These technology cycles are set out below. Figure 2.1 shows the employment potentials of three different economies. Although they may overlap in time they do not necessarily overlap in location. The growth in the new economy can be taking place fifty or 5,000 miles away from the decline in the old economy. People, *en masse*, are not that mobile so the potentials of any two economies cannot necessarily be summed together.

The employment potential of an unmechanized agricultural economy is characterized by manual labour and skills learnt on the job. There is

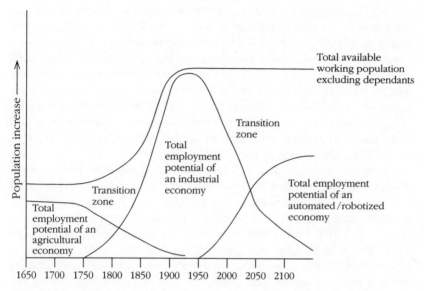

Figure 2.1 *Employment potential of economies built around different technologies*

little requirement for formal schooling and the acquisition of higher skills. When mechanization is applied to this economy, its employment potential declines dramatically, but it maintains the ability to produce the food needed by the rest of society. As the numbers employed become smaller, in line with the use of technology, the need for compensating higher skills taught through formal education rises.

The employment potential of a traditional industrial economy is mixed, as it requires manual labour that is in most respects little different from that required in an agricultural economy, but it also requires increasing acquisition of academically oriented skills learnt through formal education. Because of the almost unlimited variety of products that an industrial economy can produce, it can absorb many more people than an agricultural economy, which is tied back to the finite resource of the available land. Consequently, population numbers are able to increase dramatically. Some of the employment potential of the agricultural economy even transfers across into the industrial economy, by way of the food distribution chain. People living in towns and cities no longer grow their own food, and need to be supplied with food in varying forms, from basic ingredients to fully prepared meals. When advanced automation, computerization and ultimately total robotization is applied to the industrial economy, its employment potential declines as dramatically as it did in the agricultural economy, but it retains, for a time, the potential to meet the needs of its total population.

Historically the transition zone between the agricultural and industrial economies represents those people who were unable, for whatever reason, to make the change. Conditions for people within this zone were therefore worse than they would be for people in either the agricultural or the industrial economies. Conditions in this zone were extreme and were characterized by deep poverty and lack of opportunity. Indeed they still are for people in the Third World.

The employment potential of a fully automated and robotized economy is limited to the work that the machines are not yet able to do. This work is represented mainly by the ability to think creatively, handle abstract concepts and adapt to new ideas quickly. It requires a high level of formal education and a high degree of mental skill. It favours those individuals who possess above-average intelligence, which would suggest that the 50 per cent of the population who, by definition, possess below-average academic skills, are at risk of being excluded from this economy. Already in the most advanced industries producing the highest volumes of output there is now one robot to every ten workers.[1] Typically this applies to the automotive assembly industry. However, as this ratio narrows and other industries catch up, one of two things will happen. Either full employment will be maintained by a massive increase in output, with a corresponding massive increase in the market's ability to absorb this output, or a massive loss of jobs. If full employment is to be maintained we will have to confront the issue of depleting the earth's finite resources and the associated environmental pollution. Only 20 per cent of the world's population are at present consumers in this respect.

The use of robots is going to rise dramatically in the future. They can do jobs faster and more accurately than can humans. They can do jobs that humans find impossible to do. Figure 2.2 shows how Japanese manufacturers of robots see the growth in the use of their products in Japanese industry in the near future. When it comes down to the basics, each robot represents at least one human operator replaced, or an increase in the ability to supply without equivalent additional human involvement. The impact of 1,200,000 robots on the employment prospects of an equal number of people has got to be significant.

Today the transition zone between the industrial economy and the robotized economy is represented by those people who are unable to find a place in this new economy. Conditions within this zone are represented by lack of opportunity and slowly declining living standards. The physical well-being of people caught within this zone depends upon

Thousands

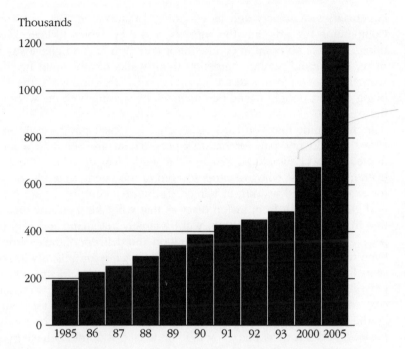

Figure 2.2 *Projected robot numbers in Japanese industry*
Source: Japan Robot Association

the ability or inclination of the remaining working population to support them, and not perceive them as a burden. One way of not being a burden is to share out the work.

The big question is whether or not we are entering the transition phase between two major technology cycles. Technology gives us both problems and opportunities. The way to solve the problems is to change our attitudes, and look at them in a new light. Instead, we seem more ready to fall back on old inappropriate attitudes, or solve them by ignoring them, on the grounds that they can't be solved anyway. Some even take the view *après moi le déluge*. We must not be afraid to question the old attitudes that we are bringing to the new technology that we are creating, and change them if they are not appropriate.

Will the competitive attitude always be right in all situations? Competition between products can drive down costs and improve quality, and this is all to the good. However, competition for limited jobs drives down wages and tears societies apart, dividing them into those who have everything and those who have nothing, even if there is enough, or the potential to create enough, for everyone. People are supposed to be the beneficiaries of society and its economic organization, not its victims. Competition rewards only the winners, and they expect to keep everything. There is no point in competing if you then have to give away the prize, but should we be competing in all walks of life? Apart from the workaholics who form a distorting minority by hoarding work, the well-being of most people would be enhanced by sharing both the work and the free time.

Is the attitude that you can't have what you can't pay for right in all cases? We do not pay for nature's gifts. There are certainly a lot of freeloaders who would sooner look at work than do it, but there are even more people who are either too old or too young to work and yet, for example, need warmth in winter. In the next century we are promised electric power from fusion reactors that will take their raw material free from sea water. The system will be largely automatic and very few people will be employed in the generation and delivery of the electricity. Even without this scientific advance, efficiency gains are still very impressive. In the five years since the UK privatized its electricity industry, payrolls are down by 50 per cent already. The largest element of marginal cost, in the system of power generation in the future, could turn out to be the profit the owners expect to take from it. Their semi-monopolistic position in this respect places them in an ideal position to behave in this way. Would we really be prepared to switch off the supply or, if it can't be switched off, waste it away, rather than provide it free, over existing powerlines, to the old people and others who need it? If you are sceptical as to whether this process has already started, then consider the figures taken from the latest relevant accounts of the companies in table 2.1. National Power, an electricity generating company, tops the list, but some of the others are doing nicely too in this context.

These companies may be the front runners, but there are many others who make 75 per cent or 50 per cent of their average wage per employee in profits. This is now recognized as one of the financial measures of success, and where the best go, the rest will try to follow.

Is the attitude that defines surplus production as the excess of supply over monetary demand correct in all cases? We are told that too much food is being produced in Europe, and the response has been to put in place a 'set aside' scheme to pay farmers not to grow food and to set aside previously cultivated land to grow back to being wild. In this way it is hoped that the agricultural industry will shrink back until supply and monetary demand again match each other. However, a quick look around the world reveals tens of millions of people starving or suffering from severe malnutrition. Even in developed countries there is an underclass of people who don't get enough to eat. Many of these are elderly people

Table 2.1 *Companies' average profits and salaries per employee*

Company	Average profit per employee (£)	Average salary per employee (£)
National Power	99,065	26,600
Guinness	38,410	19,936
Glaxo	38,611	22,548
B.A.T.	9,306	6,106
Cable and Wireless	26,391	17,478
Marks and Spencer	13,756	9,461
Abbey National	26,882	18,377
H.S.B.C. Holdings	31,119	26,008
Lloyds Bank	21,773	17,999
British Telecom	22,449	22,346

who are physically incapable of further work to earn money. Money demand is not the same as real demand. It tends to reflect only the demand of people with jobs in the formal economy, and does not match total demand to the ability to supply automatically. Why not give the people in need the set-aside money, so that they can buy the food from the farmers who want to produce it? Instead of paying the system to under-perform, by minimizing costs and bringing things back into purely monetary balance at the basest level, pay it to over-perform, and rise to the challenge. The accountant's world of book-keeping, in which money supply and money demand must always balance is, by design, blind to other options. It is a parallel world, sometimes in step with the real world and sometimes out of step with it. It is concerned with sharing out only what can be paid for, not what might be.

There are two schools of thought on the matter of jobs. One school holds that, whatever is happening at the moment, something new will come along to provide new employment opportunities to replace the ones being lost, thus everything will continue just as before. The other school of thought maintains that the technology we are now developing is specifically aimed at replacing workers with more efficient and increasingly clever technology. If this latter school of thought proves right, then we need to start the difficult process of imagining ways society can evolve to deal with the situation. First, however, let us take a futuristic look at the worst possible outcome, where technology does replace workers, nothing new comes along to provide jobs, and no-one has thought up any novel ways of dealing with the problem. The year is 2050 and we are looking into the office of a successful self-made man, whose attitudes are no different to those we see around us today in excessively competitive people.

Mr Bright started his business making security alarms twenty years earlier when he left university with a qualification in electronics and an insight into the new science of micro-passive field distortions. Using some circuitry he had designed himself he was able to measure minute changes in the earth's magnetic field caused by a living organism moving about. The technique was so sensitive that it could detect the difference between a man and a field mouse crossing a garden lawn and set off alarms accordingly.

When Bright started his business there were many other producers of security products and at first the competition was intense as they tried to squeeze out the newcomer. However, Bright's technology proved superior, and one by one the competition closed down. Unfortunately for Bright two other companies had also developed similar technology and now an industry that had once boasted hundreds of competing firms was controlled by just three very large corporations. The fact that there were three survivors was a constant irritation to the competitive Bright, because it stopped him from gaining total control of the industry. He could take on either one of his competitors and beat them, but he could not take on both and win. Still, the competition kept the government off his back and meant that he was not in breach of the anti-competition laws. The customer too was getting a good deal.

The factory area outside Bright's office was clean and quiet and dark. Lights are only required when people are employed, and as the only people who occasionally ventured on to the fully automatic shop floor were subcontract maintenance crews, there was no need for lights. The machines knew exactly what they were doing and seldom made a mistake. The only records that had to be kept in the whole manufacturing process were records of what raw materials and components had been delivered, and how many of the fully finished, packaged and ready-to-sell products had been made.

Indeed, the whole of this multi-million-pound organization was run by just a handful of highly skilled people. It was very different from even twenty years ago, when the factory had boasted a works car park, long since disused and now landscaped.

Business had been good for many years, but recently it had levelled off and showed no prospect of future growth. How could it, when the market was saturated and all but two of the competitors had been beaten? No new customers were coming forward, even though there were many more people in the world than had purchased his or his competitors' products. The unemployed in the poor areas of town could not afford security alarms, and the people living rough had no need for them. Occasionally he saw faces that he recognized as former employees amongst these disadvantaged groups. Whether they ended up as homeless, or were still able to keep a roof over their heads, depended upon their personal circumstances at the time they lost their jobs.

Bright's customers were drawn from those still employed and the rich who had something worth protecting. The rights and wrongs of the situation hardly ever entered Bright's competitive consciousness. To him life was always a battle in which there would always be winners and losers. A man's duty was to look after his own.

Still, it would be nice if there were some new customers. He had read in the electronic morning news that superconductivity had finally come of age, and that there was talk of making self-levitating cars. All the existing roads would need replacing to make them suitable for this new form of transport. That would create some new jobs and maybe some new customers too. The thought cheered him up. One article he had not noticed on the same page was about a group of students and others, who were proposing to tackle the social ills of the day by re-defining money and its role in society. To Bright, money was the reward for winning and nothing else, an attitude that had always stood him in good stead.

Bright had more money than he needed to maintain his lifestyle. It was in a secure bank account with strict instructions that it was not to be loaned out to any risky or start-up ventures. Although he was prepared to take risks in his own business, he was not prepared to take risks with his wealth. That he was saving up to purchase a grand house in a socially desirable area of town down by the lake shore where all the old, wealthy families lived. He had already put in a bid for the house that he wanted, and ownership of it would signify that he was accepted as part of the establishment. Money was for rich people who knew how to handle it. Trickle-down economics had never impressed Bright. If someone wanted to get rich then they should work for it like he had.

We don't have to invent a future to see how the wrong approach to situations by individuals, or groups of individuals, can diminish the well-being of society as a whole. Total selfish competition, combined with a misuse of technology, creates a situation of 'If I win you must lose'. What we should be looking for out of the new technology is a situation of win/win. In other words, 'If I win then so must you'. One group pursuing its self-interest at the expense of others is an enduring theme of human behaviour. History is full of examples of groups competing for dominance, and one of the most spectacular is the decline and fall of the Roman

Empire. However, we do not have to make this mistake again. We can learn if we choose to do so. H. G. Wells remarked that 'civilization is a race between catastrophe and education'. The Romans lost their race, and this is their story.

Early Rome was a republic, drawing much of its strength from a sturdy class of small farmers who made up a significant proportion of its free citizens. Corrupt, but newly enriched, tax collectors returned to Rome after pillaging the colonies. They purchased large estates and manned them with slave labour, also from the colonies. The small farmers soon found out that they could not compete with this cheaper technology and were impoverished and driven from the land. Ultimately the process provoked a civil war between the two groups, which lasted on and off for 100 years and at the end of which the democratic republic was lost. Peace was restored only by a succession of Imperial Dictators.

The rich landowners and merchants continued to grow richer and more decadent. They expanded the use of slaves, introducing them into clerical and administrative positions, which would have been the preserve of the middle class. Gradually the Roman middle class was destroyed just as the small farmers before them had been. The gap between rich and poor grew even wider.

To distract the attention of the poor from their misery, and to deflect criticism of their own conspicuous opulence, the rich gave away free bread and organized free circuses. However, when this corrupt and decadent society came up against serious opposition in the form of invading barbarian hordes, it lacked the social cohesion and strength in depth to resist successfully. It was a hollow society. The Roman Empire crumbled and with it went its achievements. There followed several centuries known as the Dark Ages.

Slaves are not robots, but robots are slaves. Can we learn how to use them for the benefit of everyone, or will we just use them to create another hollow society?

3

The Evolution of Computer Technology and its Ultimate Application as a Cost-Saving Tool

Computer technology is arguably the dominant technology of our times. It has affected most areas of our lives, but in the workplace its major impact, but not its exclusive impact, has been on so-called 'white collar' workers. These people work with information, and this is precisely what computers and their related software are designed to do as well.

Computer software offers an insight into how a modern technology can evolve. However, before we can look specifically at the software, we need to look briefly at the hardware technology that has made the evolution possible. A fuller examination of hardware technology is undertaken in a later chapter.

The evolution of computer hardware

The First Phase of computing technology was based around valves and electronic wiring, and ran from 1950 to the mid 1960s. These machines were large but lacked power and sophistication. The Second Phase of computing technology was based around transistors, and ran from the mid 1960s until 1982. These machines were still large but they were able to deliver increasing levels of computing power, and had genuine commercial potential. They were sold in large numbers to big companies and became known as 'mainframes'. The third phase of computing technology, which is still with us, is based on silicon chip technology and microminiaturization. These computers are known as 'minis' when they serve the needs of several users, and 'PCs' when they are for single users. Computers can be networked together in 'local' or 'wide' area networks, i.e. 'LANs' or 'WANs'. This technology does have limitations, but they have not been reached yet, and it is increasingly able to deliver enough computing power to make possible spectacular new applications, which will be commercially available over the next few years. Two areas of technology are proving to be bottlenecks and are holding back computer evolution at the moment. These are network bandwidths and memory access times, which are both dealt with later.

The evolution of computer software

Computer languages have evolved in line with the computing power available. First Phase computers had to be programmed in machine code. This is the lowest-level language, and is sometimes referred to as the First Generation language. It is very economic in the use of the computing power available, but it is very difficult to use. It requires the programmer to work with switches and registers, and perform every logical step in constructing an instruction for the computer to execute. It is more like advanced mathematics than English. Because of the level of detail required, it takes a long time to write programs to perform even the most simple commercially useful tasks.

Incidentally, English is the universal language of computer programming. Because the first computers were developed in Britain and America, the standard languages were also developed to use English words. The vast majority of the new programming languages are still being developed in America. Thus, just as English has become the international language of the air because of where the aeroplanes were first built, so too English has become the universal language of computer programming.

The Second Generation of computer languages evolved to make use of the increased power of the early Second Phase of computing technology, based on the transistor. These languages are referred to as Second Generation languages. Their commands group together sets of machine code instructions so that one command triggers many machine code instructions. One such language is FORTRAN, and it contains some English words that correspond to the type of command being given. There are many other 'assembler' languages. Although a vast improvement over machine code, Second Generation languages are slow and uneconomic to use by today's standards.

The real breakthrough in computer programming came with the introduction of the Third Generation languages, which took advantage of the increased computing power of the later Second Phase computers. Two of these are COBOL and BASIC, but again there are many others. These languages grouped together large numbers of machine code instructions, so that English words could be used by the programmers. These commands were the basic logical commands required to write software, such as OPEN FILE, MOVE, STORE, ADD, SAVE, PRINT, etc. This higher level of language made possible the writing of most of the commercial computer software that was used during the 1970s and 1980s, a lot of which is still in use today, under the heading of 'legacy software'.

Computing power then surged forward, with the general introduction of Third Phase silicon chip technology in the 1980s. Previously, commercial computing power had been the preserve of the 'mainframe' computer. Now it was available in greater quantity in small, relatively inexpensive, mini or deskside machines. This allowed the introduction of the highly productive Fourth Generation computer languages. These languages employ near English sentences, and it is possible for a lay person to read the program and form an idea of what it is trying to achieve. A line of a program could read 'Find the information on item number 123x and display it on the screen'. Programmers can now write applications in 10 per cent of the time it used to take to write the same thing in a Third Generation language.

However, this is not the end of the process. As well as improving efficiency, these new Fourth Generation languages also enable computer programs to be written in new ways. The lack of early computing power forced the programmers to impose the bare minimum of workload on to the computer. Consequently, they looked at what was required, simplified it and turned it into the most economical system they could. For example, a clerk takes a sales order, keys it into the computer and then electronically passes it to the stores to despatch to the customer. For this, all that is needed is a series of computer screens, one for the sales clerk to record the order, one for the storesperson to see what he has to do, and another for the storesperson to look up the stock record and see if he has enough goods to satisfy the order.

This basic functionality is too frugal for most businesses so, depending upon the precise needs of the business, extra features have to be added. These modifications might include extra fields so that the sales clerk can see if the customer has paid for the last lot of goods ordered. It might include extra fields so that the storesperson can see if any of the stock is already committed to other orders. In this way computer software becomes ever more complex, as layers of additional functionality are added to satisfy all the diverse needs of the diverse businesses that depend on the computer for their day-to-day operations. Some computer software is now so complex, with so many options, that it simply confuses the users and makes their jobs more difficult.

However, this need not be so. It arises because the originally necessary programming habits of the past have been perpetuated unnecessarily into the future. The software described above has a simple flow to it which is complicated by the addition of numerous options. Programmers trained in this procedural and structured way of designing and programming software will keep doing it in this way, and complicating themselves into an unworkable muddle unless they are retrained. They have to undergo a change of mindset, a paradigm shift, and look at the task and its solution in a completely new way. It generally takes between six months and a year for them to make the conversion. What the programmers have to do is let go of the idea that there has to be a flow in the system and that their programs are built round that flow.

What the programmers have to do is to look at all those options as 'objects' in their own right, with an existence independent of any predetermined flow. They then have to write each of those options as a separate piece of self-contained computer code, with hooks so that each one can be linked to its neighbour in any appropriate sequence, rather like children's building bricks that clip together. All these 'objects' are then held in a library. All the user has to do is go to the library and select the objects that are necessary to the task, and clip them together. This gives precisely the functionality needed, and is more efficient because the system is not carrying on line the overhead of unnecessary functionality. By the end of this century all new computer software will be written according to Object Oriented principles, or 'OO' in the jargon. Some industry analysts believe that this development will be the trigger to lower software prices. This is because once a library of reusable code has been assembled, new applications will be able to be quickly and cheaply put together. People planning careers as computer programmers should keep this in mind.

The evolution of computer technology has had a profound effect on the employment potential of most developed economies. There are three strands to this development, one each for the hardware, the software, and the impact of computer technology on the world of work in general.

Job creation in the computer hardware industry

In the First Phase of computer hardware evolution the computers were large, almost mechanical, machines. Frames had to be built to hold all the components which had to be positioned and wired up by hand, hence the name 'mainframe'. Many skilled people were required for this work. When built, these early machines required teams of operators to set the switches, load the programs, and generally look after everything. Software had to be written, and this had its own requirement for skilled people. In a modest way these First Phase computers were net creators of jobs.

The Second Phase of computer hardware evolution was a much more powerful creator of jobs within the industry. The machines, although more powerful, were still large and were still frames holding hundreds or even thousands of circuit boards that had to be assembled and tested. Now that they had a commercial application, they were built in large numbers, with a corresponding requirement for a large, growing, skilled and well-paid labour force. Giant companies such as IBM, Sperry, Burroughs, ICL, Bull, Olivetti and numerous others rose to prominence in this period. Away from the shop floor there were the head offices and the branch offices, all manned with skilled staff, to explain and sell these machines to the customers. During this period the hardware salesman was king. The machines were often expensive, costing millions of dollars, and the commissions on these sales allowed the salespeople to earn more than even the most highly paid company directors. In several companies, the salespeople's earnings were capped off at figures such as a quarter of a million pounds or dollars. Allowing for inflation, that would be today's equivalent of over a million, and many people hit the ceiling each year and simply stopped selling.

The Third Phase of computer hardware evolution is that of the silicon chip and micro-miniaturization. The computer is now automatically etched on to a piece of silicon and assembled into the smallest box possible. Portable laptop personal computers now contain as much processing power as the early mainframes and soon will contain more. All those skilled people who used to assemble the mainframe computers are no longer required and have been replaced by fewer, less skilled and lower-paid assembly workers, who slot a few mass-produced parts into plastic cases and give them a quick test to make sure that they are working.

The shopfloors of the manufacturing companies were de-skilled and downsized first, but for a time the sales and administration functions of the hardware companies remained in place to move through to market the increased volumes of mass-produced products that were coming off the automated production lines. However, as the public have become increasingly familiar with the technology, they no longer require the same selling skills of highly paid salesforces. As the computers become more 'user friendly' they no longer require the same technical support of other highly paid experts. Consequently, the giant hardware companies are now cutting their salesforces and other staff overheads by factors of 50 per cent and more. They have joined the ranks of the majority of industrial companies and are producing commodity products with limited variations. The only way they can make a profit in this highly competitive environment is to reduce their costs relentlessly by replacing people with cheaper and more reliable technology. In the space of forty years, the technology of the computer hardware industry has matured to commodity status, and it is unlikely to be a net contributor of well-paid jobs in the future.

Job creation in the computer software industry

The fortunes of the computer software industry seem to lag one stage behind that of the hardware upon which it depends. The early mainframe computers that commercial organizations purchased were lacking one vital ingredient. That ingredient was the software to process all the business information for which they were purchased in the first place. Consequently, jobs were created for large numbers of analysts, to study the needs of the organization, and programmers, to write the 'bespoke' software to address those needs. Companies suddenly found that they had a new computer department, alongside the traditional departments of sales, production, accounts, etc. The people in the new computer departments tended to see themselves as somewhat 'special', as they were dealing with a new technology that most other people hardly understood. They even spoke a technical language that differed markedly from ordinary English, and used traditional words in completely new ways. As their skills were in short supply their earnings tended to be higher than those of other workers.

However, companies soon came to realize that bespoking vast software systems for themselves was a very expensive way of doing things. Furthermore, it took time, and whilst the systems were being developed they were a cost to the business and not a contributor to efficiency or profits. A number of entrepreneurial people therefore broke away from their employers and set themselves up as small independent software houses to write ready-made packaged solutions that they could sell back to companies more cheaply than the companies could write the same things for themselves.

The first packaged software solutions started to appear on the market in the late 1970s. They proved themselves reliable and economic to use in the 1980s and now they dominate whole sectors of the market. As 'off the shelf' software has become available, companies have downsized or eliminated their 'in house' computer departments, and the bulk of the employment opportunities in computer software have moved to the independent software houses. This has represented personal disruption for the careers of individuals, but overall the growth of the software houses has produced a net increase in employment opportunity. This is for two reasons.

Firstly, the software industry is still able to find many new applications to write and sell to both the commercial user and, with the advent of the PC, to the domestic user. As computers continue to become both smaller and more powerful this trend is set to continue. Secondly, the software market is driven by a constant flow of new technology which makes previous systems obsolete. These waves of technology correspond roughly to the introduction of the new languages described previously. Software houses have to rewrite their packaged solutions in line with each new technology. Their customers, to maintain competitive advantage, have to replace their main systems every five to seven years as well. It is like painting a large steel bridge. By the time you get to the end you have to go back to the beginning and start again.

The rise of packaged software systems has given rise to other forms of employment. Some of the solutions on offer are now very complex. An integrated commercial system can address the entire needs of a substantial company. It can handle all the accounting functions right through to the production of consolidated balance sheets for multi-company groups, including foreign subsidiaries operating in different currencies. The same software will also deal with all the sales, purchasing, manufacturing, stock-holding, and distribution requirements of those companies. In addition, it will also co-ordinate the production activities of those companies, by loading production on to different factories in the most efficient way to meet changes in demand. In companies people make their whole careers within individual departments. The accountant may never visit the shop floor. The purchasing officer will be expert at his job, but have no understanding of the role of the marketing department. However, if the company is to select the best software for its overall needs, it requires someone who can see the organization as a whole, and not just through eyes that favour their own departments.

As a result of this, there has been a tremendous growth in the number of 'consultants', who specialize in advising clients on how to choose the best software for their needs. These consultants, if they are any good, have to understand the workings of the whole business to the same level as any of the individual departmental managers. A lot of these consultants are offered lucrative and very senior positions by the companies who recognize their high and broad skill sets.

Once the decision to purchase any individual software package has been made the real work then begins. The software has to be implemented. This means that the hardware and software have to be delivered and installed on site. The data from the old system has to be cleaned up and transferred across to the new system. The users have to be trained on the new system and, at some point, the old system has to be shut down without disrupting the smooth running of the company. To supervise and assist in these tasks the company will engage the services of 'project managers', who will be familiar with the software and the practical work involved. These people possess similar skill sets to those of the consultants, and many cross over to be consultants. Generally speaking, both the consultants and the project managers will be more highly paid than most of the people they are working with in the client companies. To some extent not only have the skills of the computer departments migrated to the independent software houses, so too have many of the other highly skilled people that would previously have been found in the commercial enterprises.

However, life in the software industry is not highly paid for everyone. Badly run or unfortunate companies still go bust very regularly. The writing of the software in the first instance can cost a lot of money, and many companies run out of money before they complete the task. Keeping that software up to date also takes investment. Nevertheless, the high level of potential profitability encourages fierce competition, and working hours can be as long as in any other industry. However, for the successful company the rewards can be far better than those achieved by companies supplying commodity products into mass markets. Net profits of 20 per cent on turnover are not uncommon, and annual increases in turnover of 100 per cent are regularly sustained during a successful company's growth phase.

Two factors contribute to these financial achievements. The first is the system of charging 15 per cent of the purchase price for continuing annual maintenance of the software. The customer does get benefit from this charge and so does the software house. When enough customers have purchased the software these maintenance revenues can meet most of the fixed expenses of the business. The second factor is the very low marginal cost of supplying each additional sale. All that supplying the next customer costs is, say, $10 for the tape the programs are recorded on to.

There is another factor that differentiates software from more traditional goods. Traditional goods tend to be physical things. When you buy them they become your property to use and dispose of as you want. When you have finished with them you are perfectly entitled to sell them if you can find a buyer. Cars, houses, pictures, etc. are all things for which there exists a second-hand market. This second-hand market absorbs some, maybe a lot, of the demand that would otherwise be forced into the new purchase market.

Software is different. Because it is so easy to copy software, the authors are forced to protect their intellectual property rights by never selling them outright. Most purchases of commercial software grant a 'licence to use' to a specified individual or organization. When you cease to have use for the software it is not yours to sell on to a second-hand market. You just stop using it and write off the whole cost. Software has no residual value. New users have always to buy in the new market at new market prices.

Not everyone working in the software industry is well-paid. The big money is made by those working at the leading edge, when demand is high for a new product and skills are still in short supply. The salaries today at the leading edge are not as high as those earned in the hardware industry when that was at its peak. Today salespeople selling leading-edge, complex software to commercial organizations can make £150,000 a year. Project managers advising on the implementation of that software can make £100,000 a year.

In terms of job creation the software industry is still growing. However, that growth is not as much as might first appear to be the case. The industry is being driven by technology, and each new technology wave destroys many jobs that came into existence on previous technology waves. People made redundant in the software industry can have a hard time getting back in, unless they are able to reskill themselves in the latest technology. Furthermore, not everyone is mentally or temperamentally equipped to survive in this turbulent environment.

The impact of computers on the world of work

So far we have considered the impact of computer technology from the point of view of the industry itself. However, for most people the computer revolution is more important for the effect it has had on them and their chances of employment in the economy at large.

The impact of computers started when they became commercially viable. This was from the mid 1960s onward. The decades of the 1960s and 1970s were ones of full employment, and the first effects of the new technology had little impact upon this state of affairs except, possibly, to make a further net contribution to employment.

Large companies were facing a major problem. Their people-based systems were breaking down under the volume and complexity of their operations. First let us consider the matter of volume. A company, such as an electricity company, supplying a mass market could have more than a million customers who had to be billed four times a year. That would mean the production of four million bills with all the follow-up procedure to collect and record the payments. Handled manually, this would have required thousands of sales account clerks. Just as an exercise in organization, these numbers of people would have destroyed most commercial organizations. Sorting out human error mistakes from this number of people would have tied any system up in knots. These companies needed computers to prevent the growth of employment into unmanageable numbers, not to reduce employment.

The same sort of situation also applies to the second example, that of complexity. A large and complex machine can contain thousands of parts, all of which have to be ordered or manufactured to be available to be assembled in the correct sequence at the correct time. In very large projects this involved teams of draughtsmen and material planners trying to make paper-based systems work. They could not. Parts were going missing, not arriving on time, being of the wrong design and so on. Projects were being delayed by human error and confusion, and overrunning their costs as a result. Again, computers were needed here to keep the human involvement down to manageable proportions and to handle the complexity.

In both these cases computers acted to prevent the unmanageable growth of employment and complexity but they still made a net contribution to jobs. The computers themselves created employment. They created jobs for computer operators, systems analysts, computer programmers and the management structure to supervise what was a complex operation in its own right. However, as people, and in particular management, became familiar with the technology, they started to examine the economics of maintaining large and costly computer departments. The results of this examination have already been described and have led to the use of pre-written, packaged software, purchased from independent software houses. The final blow to the internal computer department is now being delivered in the form of new computers that can run almost unattended twenty-four hours a day, without the intervention of human operatives.

The original reason for the introduction of computers was to solve the problems that were coming about through the need to employ more people than could be effectively managed. However, what can prevent a growth in numbers can also effect a reduction in numbers as the technology becomes more refined and reliable. The original investment in computers was made out of necessity. With that problem solved, subsequent investment in computers has been, and still is being, justified on the basis of a reduction in costs. If there are two ways of doing a job and one involves people and costs £100,000, and the other involves a computer and costs £75,000, then the computer will be purchased and people will be made redundant. It is in the interests of software writers to make the computer more sophisticated in its abilities. It is in the interests of the computer salesperson to justify a client investing in a new computer, to be able to show a saving in costs, and this usually involves reducing the wages bill. If it does not involve an actual reduction in existing staff numbers, then the alternative justification will be the ability to take on new business without having to increase the number of people employed.

The nub of the problem is that computers process information more efficiently than people can. The first effects of this were, as above, on the jobs of people processing relatively simple information. Now computers are able to process complex information, and this is having its effect on the more senior levels of management. One purpose of management is to collect, collate, and present information in ways that allow decisions to be taken. The process of collecting and collating complex information has been done, out of necessity, by highly educated people who themselves formed some of the layers of management. Now there is Executive Information Systems software, or EIS, and another chance to eliminate the human element.

EIS software works in this way. When company data is stored in a standard database on a computer it is stored in a structured way. Pieces of information are linked one to another, according to common usage, so that they can be recalled more speedily. For example, a customer name will be linked to an address, telephone number, and other related information. In daily use it would not be usual to want to know a name without this data. However, someone might want to know how many customers the company has in each of a series of towns. In the standard database the information could be obtained, but only with the rest of the linked data being recalled as well. The position gets more complicated if the data on the number of customers is to be compared to some other data, such as the amount of money spent on advertising in each of those towns. This advertising data could itself be linked to other data such as sales of specific products. Thus to get at the data required in the first place, work has to be done to strip away the unwanted information, so that the comparison can be made. An EIS database works by breaking all these links, in the jargon 'denormalizing', and storing each piece of data as a separate entity. Using an enquiry or query language a user can now interrogate the database for the precise information needed and compare it to any other information that might be of interest.

This type of activity is called 'slicing' the data, after the way doctors can use powerful magnetic imaging machines to take pictures that are slices through the patient's head or body, and which can reveal abnormalities. In the same way, executives can slice through and compare company data that would previously have kept a skilled person busy for days, writing special programs to get at the facts and compiling the necessary reports. The managing director no longer needs a university graduate as a research assistant. He can ask the computer directly.

This analysis of the impact of computer technology has looked at the situation from three angles. Two of those angles now point to a reduction in actual or potential employment and only one points to an increase in employment potential. Computer technology in the form of commercial systems is only one of the ways that computing science is being applied to reducing costs by profit-driven organizations. Computing technology is also being embedded into machine tools, railway signalling systems, cash dispensing systems and much more. This technology usually leads to better products, safer systems or more convenience. The consumer benefits, but the worker loses his job. Are they two different people or are they one and the same?

It is sobering to think that everything that we are able to do with computers today we could do in our imaginations twenty years ago. What was lacking then was the computing power to drive the applications. Most of the things we imagine computers will be able to do in the future will happen when the hardware becomes available. If we imagine factories controlled by computers and manned by robots, then it will come to pass if we apply our research development efforts in this direction. A jobless society is within our reach.

4

Progress is Three Per Cent

_____

Computers represent a whole new technology 'kicking in', but the search for greater efficiency and competitive advantage is also a gradual process of steady improvement in the use of existing technologies and organizational methods. Average efficiency is growing every year across whole economies by an estimated 3 per cent. This is a widely accepted figure if a little difficult to measure accurately. What it means is that every year up to 3 per cent of the jobs in an economy are disappearing and will not be replaced, unless output in the economy grows at 3 per cent or more to compensate. We have to grow to stand still in terms of output and jobs. The jobs currently most susceptible to elimination are the highly paid manual jobs, where people are working with machines, and well-paid white-collar jobs, where people are working with information. The jobs least susceptible to elimination are the low-paid menial tasks, where it is not worth while putting in the investment if there is a surplus of low-paid people and, in contrast, the highly skilled jobs, at the leading edge of innovation, requiring high standards of education. If we take a hypothetical situation where there is no growth in the economy, but efficiency eliminates jobs at a steady 3 per cent per year, then in less than thirty years there could be no jobs left in whole sectors of the economy.

The figure 3 per cent is an average. If a whole new phase of technology kicks in, then it could jump to 5 or 10 per cent. In a technologically stable economy it could be as low as zero. According to the Confederation of British Industry, productivity in UK manufacturing grew at 6 per cent in 1993. The Engineering Employers Federation predicted that for 1994–5 output in the engineering sector of the British economy would rise by 3 per cent and at the same time employment would fall by 3 per cent. Banking and insurance used to be sleepy, if profitable, areas of the economy where gentlemen did business in traditional ways that had not changed for decades. This is no longer so, and enormous job losses are going to be suffered by these sectors over the next few years. The last bastion of traditional ways in the British economy is the Government and its Civil Service. More than half a million jobs are at risk if new technology is allowed in there. The same will apply to any other nation because technology does not recognize national borders. Perhaps surprisingly, one of the countries which could suffer most in this respect is the USA which has a very bureaucratic approach to government administration.

If the Japanese get too many favourable references in relation to efficiency, it is because they have earned them. Over the last half century it has been their willingness to embrace new thinking that has enabled them to perform an economic miracle of outstanding proportions. Out of the top fifty industrial companies (not businesses) in the world, seventeen are Japanese, fifteen are American, and the whole of western Europe can only muster eighteen.[1] The position of this small Pacific island country is even more impressive when the top ten companies in the world are compared. Six of them are Japanese, three are American and one is European. In fact Japanese companies occupy the first, second, third, fourth, fifth and ninth positions. All of this from an economy that was in ruins less than fifty years ago. It has been their willingness to break with traditional management thinking, particularly in the area of manufacturing, that has allowed them to prosper ahead of their western rivals. It is their ideas that the West is now picking up and using in order not to be destroyed in the global race for economic prosperity. What the West has not yet picked up on is the fact that the Japanese way is not that of short-term capitalism for short-term profits. It is a highly competitive, if unspoken, long-term strategy for the benefit of all its citizens.

In contrast, the Anglo-Saxon route to efficiency is economics at its most individualistic. At its worst, the company is seen by its owners as a fortress surrounded by hostile suppliers and customers whose only ambition is to overcharge or underpay. The *raison d'être* of the company is to wrest as much money away from suppliers and customers as possible and pile it up within its fortress walls to the benefit of the owners. To this end negotiations with suppliers are confrontational, concentrating on obtaining the lowest possible price regardless of how that is achieved. Negotiations with customers are less than honest, and are about delivering as little as possible for as high a price as possible. Within the fortress walls all is not happy either, because the workforce is seen as a cost too, which has to be driven down. Everything is reduced to money, and efficiency is measured only by how much profit is made. Quality, value, service, recognition of effort and future investment play only a small part. This is the company of the exploiter, aided and abetted by short-sighted accounting definitions of profitability. This is the Victorian approach to capitalism that has lived too long in the minds of western business men and allowed the Japanese to capture so much of the West's markets.

However, whilst we have a lot to learn from the more successful economies of the Far East, there are lessons that emerging economies need to learn from us as they become richer. It is often argued that western industry is uneconomic in its labour costs because firms have to carry extra labour costs in the form of benefits such as sick pay, pensions arrangements, maternity leave and so on. This is in comparison to companies in emerging regions where the social dimension of employment policy is not yet developed. Consequently, there is a lobby in the USA and the UK for the removal of these internalized social obligations. However, society can't have it both ways. If costs that are now internalized to the company are to be externalized to society, then they still have to be met somehow, and the only way to meet them is through taxation, which is paid by the firms or by the employees. Either way, they are still costs that a civilized society has to bear and that will be reflected in the cost of its products. The alternative is to leave large sections of the population without cover. Take the case of medical care. In the UK this is supported through general taxation and a National Health Service. In America it is supported through medical insurance paying for private healthcare. However, most workers cannot afford to pay the high premiums, and so traditionally these are paid by the employer. Blue Cross and Blue Shield (health insurance) is the biggest item of supply on General Motors' purchase ledger, not, as might be expected, steel or other automotive parts.

Winston Churchill said that the bad employer will always drive out the good employer unless measures are taken to stop that from happening. The suspicion has to be that the lobby from certain business people in the West to externalize the costs of employment is intended as a one-way affair. They want to be rid of the costs and do not want them back in the disguise of higher corporate or personal taxation. In other words, they are prepared to see the bad employment practices of certain emerging economies drive out the good working practices of the mature western producers. Japan has shown that this need not be so. Japanese industry internalizes more social cost in its labour bill than do most western companies. They are famous for their cradle to grave care of their workforces. This must put considerable strains on company finances, but the benefits that loyalty and the long-term development of internal skills are delivering for them are so much the greater. It remains to be seen if the more socially responsible employment practices of Japan and Germany can stand up to the competition of cheaper labour costs from low-waged economies in both the developing world and, unfortunately, sometimes the developed world.

Modern techniques for greater efficiency

Just In Time (JIT)

This is one of the new concepts that is surrounded by mystery but in reality is very simple. Just In Time is a Japanese concept and is all about being better organized. To be responsive to the customer's needs you have to be able to deliver what he wants as soon as he wants it. In today's competitive environment, companies that can't respond in this way lose orders. It means that usually within a few days, or sometimes within a few minutes, of the customer making up his mind the company has to be able to deliver. This is not an easy thing to do, particularly when the product is complex and contains hundreds of components sourced from dozens of suppliers.

One way would be to carry stocks of all the components so that each order, no matter how varied, could be filled from stock off the shelf. However, the cost of this would be horrific. The accountants can rightly point out that the costs of carrying stocks of this magnitude will put any company out of business. The only other way to cater for all the combinations of customer choice is for companies to be able to re-specify their requirements to their suppliers at the last minute, or Just In Time. This is an enormous logistical exercise to organize, and typically it takes years to put into place.

However, it has been done extensively by the Japanese. In their best organized automobile factories, it is possible for a customer to order a car two weeks in advance and change his mind about the specification up to two hours before the car commences its journey down the production line. Goods are constantly being delivered by outside suppliers to the precise location on the production line where their particular contributions, matching a customer's requirements, are scheduled to be fitted. They are unloaded from the delivery vehicles in the correct sequence, ready to be fitted on to the partly assembled vehicles as they pass by. The news is good for the accountants as well. The amount of lineside stock is usually enough for one or two hours' production only, so work in progress stock is minimal. Cars are being made to customer order and not to stock, so the value of finished cars held in stock too is minimal.

These supply chains that tie companies together into efficient units of total supply for Just In Time manufacturing are only possible in a world of long-term co-operation and partnership. This is where the Japanese emphasis on building and maintaining relationships is all-important. This is in total contrast to the Victorian view of individual capitalist entrepreneurs fighting both customers and suppliers for the available profits. JIT is too fragile to survive in a world seeking short-term advantages through shifting alliances. JIT relies on a level of co-operation that, until recently, was alien to the thinking of most Western management. JIT relies on the individual players realizing that they are in reality a part of a system which, when in place, can deliver quality products on time at half the price of their disjointed and internally warring Western competitors.

Eliminating set-up times

A phenomenon referred to as 'set-up time' has dominated much of our Western management thinking. Maybe it is more accurate to say that it has not dominated our thinking openly, because although it was there and had tremendous implications, it was taken for granted much of the time and it was dismissed as an insoluble problem. Set-up time is nothing complicated, but it comes at the start of most manufacturing processes and so influences everything that follows on. Machines or production lines have to be set up correctly for each product they are going to produce. Sometimes this is only a matter of a few minutes if, for example, it only involves changing a simple drill bit. However, it can sometimes take several days to change over the dies on large stamping machines that press out products from pieces of metal. As these long set-up times were suffered by all, there was no pressure to do much about them, and industry used to accept them as a fact of life. The herd instinct of thinking had set in.

The implications of accepting set-up times of, not untypically, three days have been profound. A machine out of use for three days has a major impact on company costs and recovery rates. It is the same as having to suffer a complete factory shutdown but with all the costs still running against the business. A perfectly logical reaction to this has been to avoid changing over production runs as much as possible. Once the pain of setting up for a production run has been suffered, the natural thing would seem to be to make as much of whatever it is as possible, before losing another three days setting up for the next product.

These large-batch runs have several consequences. The goods made have to be stored, and that costs money and ties up working capital. If a fault is later discovered in the batch, then the cost of scrapping the batch and starting again is heavy. If the market moves on before the batch is sold so that it becomes obsolete, then this too is a heavy write-off cost. If the amount made is used up before the next batch is due to be made, then the customer either has to wait or, more likely, takes his business elsewhere. If the product feeds into another process, then the whole of that process can be brought to a standstill until fresh supplies are available. However, despite all these drawbacks, no-one really saw that there was a problem and therefore the need for a solution. It was the same pain for everyone, another inconvenient fact of life. No one saw it, that is, until the Japanese looked at it with a different attitude.

No-one had told the Japanese that set-up times could not be changed. They looked at the totality of the manufacturing process and imagined how things might be ordered in a perfect world. Then the problem became obvious. They looked at the whole system, of which set-up times were just a small part, and saw how a wrong attitude at the beginning of the process was distorting everything that followed on, and that solving the problem would bring them a tremendous competitive advantage. Management and workers studied the problem as a team. Any time that could be shaved off those three days was taken into account, no matter how small. Some of the ideas were just plain obvious, such as assembling all the necessary tooling and work crews to be ready to start the changeover the minute the machine stopped, instead of waiting till the beginning of the next shift. Progress was not spectacular but it was steady. After several months the set-up time was down to two days. After two years of small incremental improvements it was down to two hours, and in this example the new target is to reduce it to a matter of minutes.

The overall effect of tackling this problem of set-up time has been to completely revolutionize management thinking, and the Japanese who pioneered the idea have been the first to benefit. Their factories can now make what is needed when it is needed. The process is part of Just in Time manufacturing. Set-up time has ceased to be a problem because it has been fixed and not ignored. There is now no need to make large quantities of a product at any one time and to store it. Scrap is minimal, because mistakes are identified as they are happening and corrected immediately. Obsolete products are not manufactured, and the customer gets what he wants when he needs it. Taken together, the overall savings and increases in productivity, inherent in the above improvements to the manufacturing process, can be worth anything up to 20 per cent of the price of an item. This margin has been put to good use by the Japanese

Table 4.1 *Engineering sector performance*

	Average performance	Top 25%	Top 10%
Delivery reliability	87.0%	98.0%	100%
New product introduction over last 5 years (new product/ product range)	3.0%	15.0%	62.0%
Scrap rate	2.7%	0.5%	0.3%
Manufacturing added-value per direct manufacturing employee (£000)	61.0	65.0	90.0
Total stock turns	9.0	11.0	18.0
Capacity used for change-overs	9.7%	3.3%	1.0%
Average component set-up time (mins)	84.0	16.0	10.0
Absenteeism	3.2%	2.0%	1.0%

Source: Cranfield School of Management and *Management Today*

in winning new markets, and displacing less efficient producers from markets that they had come to think of as their own. In this example very little new technology is required, just new attitudes. Fewer workers are able to produce more products more efficiently and the improvement is continuing. The Japanese do not mind sharing this knowledge, because they reckon that by the time their rivals have mastered today's ideas, they will have moved ahead by at least three years.

In this matter the Japanese may be a little too optimistic. The best companies in the UK are now putting up impressive performances. Unfortunately, faced with world competition, only the best companies are likely to survive. The 65 per cent who are not making the grade face an uncertain future. Table 4.1 makes the point for the engineering sector of the British economy.

Empowering the workers

The fortress company trusts no-one, not even its own workers. Everything has to be supervised and authorized. There are still isolated instances in some large companies where senior executives have to sign off all expenditure over, say, £100 because no-one else is trusted to do so. Typical of this culture is the following scenario that is still all too common in many companies.

A shop floor worker has to tell a supervisor that some new parts are needed. The supervisor checks and signs off the request, and passes it through to the purchasing department. A buyer then telephones various suppliers and negotiates the best price. He raises a purchase order and sends it to the supplier allotted to the business. The supplier then sends back an acknowledgement. The goods eventually arrive at the goods receiving bay. As the supplier probably won the business on price, the goods have to be checked to make sure that they are of the right quality and not substandard. A goods receiving note is raised confirming that quantity and quality are acceptable and this is sent back to the buyer to await the arrival of the supplier's invoice.

The storeman then puts the goods into stock and enters up the stock records. The shop floor worker is then able to go to the stores and withdraw what he needs to complete his work. When the invoice arrives the buyer compares it to the goods received note and sorts out any discrepancies. The invoice is then passed through to the accounts section where it is entered on to the ledger. After the passage of time agreed in the credit terms, a list is produced of all the items to be paid on this cheque run, and is passed to the chief accountant for approval. This is given (or refused), and a cheque is then raised and sent to the supplier. Does anyone recognize this as the company they are working for?

Many tens of thousands of people owe their jobs to this way of working, but compare it to how some world class companies now do business. They are open with their suppliers, and involve them in their business planning, telling them how much of their product will be needed each month for the next two or three years. In return they expect an absolute commitment to quality at an agreed price. All supplies will therefore be inspected by the supplier before shipment, and all deliveries will be on time and totally free from defects. With the security of the knowledge that they are dealing with a business partner, and not a cheating competitor, the ordering process can now be transformed. In one real example, a factory taking this approach with electrical components that it builds into its own finished product, has them delivered direct to the production line in reusable boxes. When the box is empty the worker concerned simply folds the box flat and puts it in the post back to the supplier. The box is then filled by the supplier and returned to that same worker, directly at the production line, without going through inspection or goods inwards stores. In the meantime, the worker has told the accounts department what has happened, and at the end of the week a cheque is automatically sent to the supplier for the goods at the negotiated price. It is taken for granted that the right goods arrived at the right time and that they were of the right quality.

At the end of the day the workers report, by keying into a computer, the number of units built during their shift, and a process of backflushing takes place. Backflushing simply means that the computer can perform a calculation along the lines that 'if we have made so many units then we must have used the following components in the following quantities'. It can then retrospectively fill in all the necessary records to record the transactions that have taken place. This is lean manufacturing in operation, and it pays dividends.

This system requires that there be trust and not antagonism between customer and supplier and their respective workforces. This only builds up over time as a result of a long-term relationship. It is in contrast to the short-term thinking that has dogged Western management, but the benefits cannot be ignored. The extra care required to be exercised by the supplier may actually mean a slightly higher per unit price than previously, but the saving on total purchase price, including the administrative overheads, is as high as fifty per cent. The same number of workers can produce more products more cheaply without a negative impact on their wages. If a company is expanding, wages should be one of the last aspects to be considered for cutting back. There are much larger savings to be made elsewhere. The story can be different for the managers and supervisors who may have seen themselves as indispensable to their employers.

Flat management structures

As soon as workers are trusted, and empowered to make decisions without constant reference to supervisors, then those layers of shop floor supervision automatically become redundant. The same lesson can be applied to management structures. As soon as junior management is trusted and empowered to make substantive decisions, then supervising layers of senior management automatically become redundant. The typical organizational pyramid structure of several layers becomes flattened into just two or three layers. The man on the shop floor can talk to the man at the top because he is no longer remote. In a Japanese company the management may even wear the same clothes and eat in the same dining room as everyone else. The man at the top can see what is happening on the shop floor and can no longer claim ignorance when things go wrong. The whole organization becomes more responsive, and that alone is a significant competitive advantage in today's fast-moving environment.

The removal of several layers of management takes out significant payroll costs. Expensive offices too can be vacated and their costs eliminated. It also takes out several layers of promotion, and with them the distraction of playing politics to gain promotion up those plentiful rungs of the corporate ladder. The company becomes more focused on serving the customer and more aware of what it is about.

Redundancy has long been a feature of shop floor life, but now it is affecting the middle management, middle income layers of the economy. White-collar workers are joining blue-collar workers in the unemployment figures. In some cases managers are being offered the opportunity to retrain as shop floor workers instead of being made unemployed. In the UK between 1990 and 1994 the number of unemployed white-collar workers and managers has risen threefold. Job insecurity amongst the middle classes is now a fact of life.

Total Quality Management

The Japanese took Total Quality seriously from early on. The concept of Total Quality is an American one, put forward by an American called W. Edwards Deming. He tried to get his ideas accepted in America but was turned down. After the Second World War the American factories were working flat out to supply the world, and quality was not as important as quantity. He went to Japan where he was taken seriously, and now there is an annual prestigious award in his name, given out to the best performing Japanese companies for improvements in quality.

The Japanese decided that there was no reason why every car leaving their factories should not be perfect, hence the name Total Quality. It did not happen overnight; changes to people's thinking processes take time to take effect. At first, finished cars were inspected before they left the factories, and the faults were corrected. This is an easy but very expensive way of doing things. Therefore the faults were traced back down the production lines to where they occurred and the causes corrected there. If the fault was traced back to an outside supplier, then that factory was visited and told to put the matter right and so on. Eventually there was no need to inspect the finished cars, because at every stage of the manufacture and assembly processes, quality-conscious workers automatically inspected their work and that of others. The final inspection process could therefore be done away with and the money that it had cost thus eliminated. At this point quality becomes free.

The cost of not having Total Quality is hidden until it is searched out. Take the assembly of a piece of electrical equipment that has 100 small components on a circuit board, which is fitted into a bigger assembly. If just one of those components is faulty the whole product will malfunction.

If the component is one of a faulty batch then the problem is so much the greater. The whole batch may have to be scrapped. The time spent isolating the fault and rectifying it is usually not properly recorded. It is too painful to record all the wage costs and other overheads associated with a mistake. It is far easier just to record the cost of the faulty component. This scrap value may be pennies only, and conveniently covers up the mistake. If the full costs are recognized their impact can be dramatic. Most companies probably only average a 10 per cent profit on turnover. The true hidden cost of faults and scrap can easily be 2.5 per cent of turnover or a quarter of a company's profits.

The British car industry used to be plagued by poor quality, which it actually allowed to be shipped to its customers. Untypically, a major German car producer is reported to have a similar problem at the time of writing. Only 20 per cent of their production is passing final inspection as Right First Time. The other 80 per cent is having to be held back and the faults corrected by hand. The cost to the company is massive and is putting a strain on its resources that it need never have suffered. Poor quality creates jobs that are not sustainable in the long term and can destroy a company.

This realization of the true costs of not doing it right has made companies adopt policies of Right First Time and Better by Design. The world of management science is full of catch phrases. Right First Time means what it says and the whole supply chain, with its multitude of manufacturing and assembly processes, is examined, to exclude the possibility of mistakes and faults creeping in. Scrutiny of this sort usually also leads to all sorts of other inefficiencies being identified and eliminated.

Total Quality is an attitude of mind. It is about taking the whole process of manufacturing a product or providing a service seriously. It is about taking a professional attitude to industry and treating it as a scientific process, to be studied with as much dedication as any other scientific discipline. It is about spending time seeing if a piece of wire in a television set can be shortened by a few centimetres, or if a panel on a car door can be held in place by three screws instead of four screws. Hardly exciting stuff, when fiction portrays high-powered executives racing between meetings, doing deals, or heroically solving problems at the last minute that threaten to shut the factory down. Fire fighting, as it is called, is much more exciting than the pedestrian task of planning in detail so that things don't go wrong. The wire saved, or the screw not used, are insignificant in themselves but, spread over millions of units sold, contribute to the competitive edge.

Total Quality is not a process that starts and finishes like an election campaign. It is a process that has no end. It carries on relentlessly, looking for ways to improve product quality and drive down costs. Targets for improvement are set and, when achieved, they are replaced by more ambitious targets for the next year. In a Just In Time supply chain the lead company will require its suppliers to find ways of delivering the same products to higher quality specifications at lower cost each year. Product improvement is relentlessly pursued, and any competition that can't keep up is destroyed by the better product. Companies seeking only above-average, short-term profits, usually quit these areas of activity, and in so doing they also quit the volume markets.

If it is right to apply the principles of Total Quality Management to industry, then might it not also be right to apply those same standards to the evolution of society? If it is right to work in an environment where the philosophy is one of continuous improvement, it must surely be appropriate to live in an environment where there is also continuous improvement for everyone. When you come to accept something as powerful as Total Quality Management into one area, it is difficult not to apply it in other areas. The application of Total Quality Management principles, suitably modified, to national life would have some interesting results. Under this philosophy any lowering of standards in any area, or for any group, would be totally unacceptable, and ways would be found to prevent it from happening. Experience from industry strongly suggests that ways would indeed be found if only we had the political will.

Better by Design

Up to 50 per cent of the cost of manufacturing a product is either designed in, or designed out, at the design stage of a product's evolution. Complexity is one factor making for mistakes. The more components there are, the more processes there are, then the more likelihood there is that something will go wrong. Today products are made Better by Design. This means designing them with fewer components, simpler to make, easier to use and less likely to break. Despite the jokes, modern products are more reliable and last longer, and there are fewer jobs for repair men both at the factory and in the after market.

The less that goes into a product, the less the raw materials cost. Fewer components take less time to assemble, and work in progress is less, as goods spend less time on the shop floor and move out to the customers faster. Physically smaller products can be made in smaller factories. Fewer components mean that the product weighs less and so costs less to transport. Simplified, functional products can be sold for less and fewer workers can produce more of them. The cumbersome mechanical products of the industrial revolution are being replaced by devices that achieve the same ends, but which consume fewer raw materials with far fewer people being needed to manufacture them.

Mean Time Between Failure (MTBF)

The industrial revolution was a mechanical revolution. Mechanical devices have moving parts, and there is friction between moving parts, so they wear out and have to be replaced. The new technology is increasingly solid-state in which there are no moving parts and so there is nothing to wear out. The mean time between failure of solid state products far exceeds that for mechanical devices. They last longer, need less maintenance, can be made smaller and more cheaply, and fitted in more applications. Many companies today still make their money not on supplying the original mechanical product, but on supplying spares and maintenance over the life of the product. They have, to borrow an agricultural term, field service engineers who will visit customer sites and make repairs. As solid state takes over from mechanical we get more reliability and fewer jobs. Computers are one area where solid-state technology has nearly completely replaced all mechanical technology and consequentially the role of the computer engineer in servicing and repairing computers is much diminished. Hewlett Packard, for example, quotes MTBF on some of its components of 100,000 hours. In layman's language that is approximately twelve and a half years.

More efficient by choosing the correct way to measure success

In general terms the western mindset tends to take an atomistic approach to problem solving, whereas the eastern mindset takes a holistic approach. (Western medicine concentrates on treating the specific illness, eastern medicine treats the whole person.) Is a company, or a society, no more than the sum of its parts, or is it the company, or society, that gives meaning to the parts and adds something extra?

If a company is no more than the sum of its parts, then the better the individual performances are, the better the company will perform. However, if too much weight is placed on this approach it can give rise to mistaken measures of performance, such as piece work and individual performance bonuses, and too much reliance on incentives to encourage them. Is it really necessary to pay a few 'high-profile' executives astronomical bonuses for doing what is, after all, their jobs? If these bonuses are linked to the share price performance, then they will cause the company's development to be distorted by short-term measures to raise profits to the detriment of long-term growth and development.

Take the example of what we now recognize as a badly organized factory. The buyers are motivated to get the lowest prices, so they order too much raw material in order to maximize the benefit of bulk discounts. The machine operators are paid by the number of parts they produce. They queue (hoard) raw materials in front of their machines so that they will be busy for weeks and never be short of work. The sales department is rewarded by commission paid on the number of sales they make in a week, so they over-order from the shop floor to make sure that they always have enough in stock to catch every potential customer.

In each case the employees are efficiently and correctly fulfilling their objectives, even though the enterprise is slowly going broke through carrying too much stock at every stage of its manufacturing process. What these individual measures of success fail to show is how each employee is part of a system that works best when it flows. Purchasing should only order what is needed. The machine operators should only produce what is needed. Sales should only order what they can reasonably expect to sell. The whole system should flow and be responsive to changes in demand as a team. The erroneous individual bonuses need replacing with a group bonus, based on the performance of the whole enterprise. By looking at the whole, and considering where the parts fit into the whole, the Japanese have created factories where efficiency is based on harmonious flows, or Just in Time manufacturing. These factories are more efficient than anything western industry has managed to come up with.

National and cultural differences

Different national cultures have thrown up different management structures, attitudes and measures of success. America is the spiritual home of capitalism. Historically the American business hero has been the self-made man who had the courage to 'go for it' and establish a business. Success is the objective, and profit is the reward and tangible proof of success. In recent years profits have been easier to generate on Wall Street than they have been to generate on the factory floor. Businesses have been bought and sold, broken up, and rearranged to provide gains for the financiers and speculators. It has not been fashionable of late to spend time building up businesses from scratch, and much of America's manufacturing potential has been lost or transferred abroad.

British business shares many of the attitudes and mistakes of its American counterpart, tempered by a more cautious attitude towards risk. Cautious accountants hold positions in British industry that would be occupied by aggressive business school graduates in American companies. An accountant, when presented with an improvement to a product, will ask, 'how much will it cost and how long is the payback?' Normally if the cost is not paid back quickly, then an accountant will not recommend that the money be spent, and the improvement will not be made. An article in the *Financial Times*[2] points out that UK companies are still looking for payback periods of two to three years and returns on capital of 20 per cent. Michael Heseltine, the British Government minister with responsibility for Trade and Industry, told the 1994 Confederation of British Industry conference that he had an example of a 30 per cent return on capital being demanded. On the face of it, this could explain why Japanese gross fixed capital formation as a percentage of GDP is 28 per cent, whilst the UK manages only 14 per cent. On paper, the best way of making a profit out of an existing product is to keep selling it whilst spending nothing on it. In the jargon, milk it like a cash cow.

Japanese business appears to be working to a different agenda. It wants to make profits, but sees no problem in making those profits more modestly out of manufacturing. It plans in the long term and not the short term. There is no long term for a business if the business stands to be sold, taken over and broken up. No worker can give loyal and lifetime service to a business that cannot guarantee lifetime employment in return. Businesses are part of the Japanese social fabric. They are respected and preserved as the means to generating future prosperity. Hostile take-overs are unknown on the Japanese stock exchange. Foreign corporate raiders, flush with success and money from their antics on Wall Street, have tried to buy into Japanese companies on a hostile take-over basis, but they have been frozen out and forced to retreat nursing losses. None have succeeded. Their short-term goal of 'unlocking shareholder value' is seen as nothing more than eating next year's seed corn.

This difference in attitude between Japanese companies and their western counterparts has a profound effect on corporate decisions. Japanese companies look to long-term competitive success as the way of delivering present and future profits. Product improvements are not weighed against the cost of making them, as they would be by a British accountant. They are weighed against the cost of not making them. Changing a production line, or method of working, to improve product quality by just 1 per cent, may not be justified by payback analysis or any other measure of the effort required. However, if it is made nonetheless, then that product becomes a little better in the eyes of the consumer. Keep making these trivial improvements, and after a year the product might be 5 per cent better than the competition. If the competition's eyes are focused on its short-term profits and not product quality then it may well not spot the growing threat. After three years of stealthy improvement the difference will be a substantial 15 per cent, and that can put a competitor out of business. This is just what has happened. Japanese industry's increased profits are coming through by virtue of increased market share, taken from western companies too mean to put in the necessary investment to keep themselves competitive. Continuous improvement is here to stay.

If there is a hidden agenda to what the Japanese are doing then it could be this. Efficiency is going to increase and that means that fewer people are progressively going to make more and more products. If they are promising lifetime employment to their workforce in return for their loyalty, then their ever increasing output has to be sold somewhere. This can only be done by controlling an ever increasing share of the available markets. Japan is a small country of 100 million people. The population of the USA is 250 million. The population of the European Economic Community is 350 million. The five largest industrial companies in the world are Japanese. Out of the top fifty industrial companies, eighteen are European, fifteen are American and seventeen are Japanese. The figures might just be speaking for themselves. If there are going to be fewer jobs in the future, then the Japanese might just be planning that they be filled by Japanese workers. Already 40 per cent of Japanese industrial production is accounted for by products that did not exist thirty years ago. Additionally, a higher proportion of the Japanese workforce is employed in hi-tech industry than that of any other nation.[3] They are not only showing us how to succeed in the JIT-oriented commodity product markets, they are leading the way in the emerging hi-tech industries as well.

The world is changing very rapidly. It is becoming smaller, as transport and communications improve to the point that nowhere is more than a telephone call away, or a short air flight away. People from different cultures simply have different attitudes to life. They have different ways of looking at the world. We mix and compete on a day-to-day basis not really understanding each other. In these situations entrenched attitudes are dangerous. We need to keep our minds open to new ideas so that we can see and grasp new opportunities as they come along. In the last few decades it is the Japanese who have challenged our Western way of doing business. One day China and India will be major economic powers. Their people account for nearly half the world's population. Their impact on the way business will be done will be even greater. We don't yet know what their business strategies will be.

However, what we do know is that, since the signing of the GATT, competition is now global. We have to compete with the best in the world even in our own market place. Continuous improvement is here to stay. Any country that is not improving efficiency by 3 per cent a year is falling behind world class manufacturing standards. Any country that is not increasing its output and growing at 3 per cent a year is failing to replace those good jobs that it is losing to efficiency. Very few, if any, western countries have succeeded in achieving, let alone maintaining, this level of growth. Most western countries have experienced rising levels of unemployment and an expansion in part-time, low-paid, fringe employment.

Further reading

Belasco, James A., *Teaching the Elephant to Dance* (Crown Publishers Inc., New York, 1990).

Goldratt, Eliyahu M. and Cox, Jeff, *The Goal* (Gower, Aldershot, 1990).

Harman, Roy L., *Reinventing the Factory* (The Free Press, New York, 1992).

Maurer, Rick, *Caught in the Middle* (Productivity Press, Cambridge, Ma., 1992).

Nayak, Ranganath P. and Ketteringham, John M., *Breakthroughs* (Mercury Books, London, 1987).

Schmidt, Warren H. and Finnigan, Jerome P., *The Race Without a Finish Line* (Jossey-Bass Inc., San Francisco, 1992).

Shonk, James H., *Team Based Organisations* (Business One Irwin, Homeward, Il., 1992).

Stack, Jack, *The Great Game of Business* (Doubleday Currency, New York, 1992).

Walton, Mary, *Deming Management at Work* (G.P. Putnam's Sons, New York, 1990).

Wheatley, Malcolm, *Understanding JIT* (Hodder & Stoughton, Sevenoaks, Kent, 1992).

5

Can Everything be Saved?

When you sell software to industrial companies as I do, you get to see first hand what is going on and how companies are reacting to change. In the previous chapter I referred to some of the improvements that are becoming commonplace. I saw the problem of 'set-up' times in a company that stamped out turbine blades for use in jet engines. JIT is now an everyday occurrence with suppliers of components to the automotive industry. There are specific software modules specially written for these companies, so that they can work to the JIT schedules handed down by the main assembly plants. Total Quality is a requirement in many industries, and a prerequisite to doing business with other quality-conscious enterprises. Even software companies have their own quality scheme, and in this context I am a certified quality auditor.

The process of winning a contract to supply software that can cost a company anything between £50,000 and £1 million usually begins with the receipt of an Invitation to Tender, followed by a site visit to see first hand the problems that need to be addressed. Unfortunately some of the companies you get to visit, although doing their best and even doing everything right, are probably not going to prosper whatever they do. The examples that follow are based on real companies that have been generalized because they are typical of the challenges that face us today.

Example 1 concerns a traditional engineering company making essential, low-tech, standard, turned parts that find their way into all manner of everyday items. The products can only command commodity-type prices, and the company is under constant pressure to further reduce its prices as part of the relentless pressure from its main customers, who in turn want to stay price-competitive. There is little, other than price, to differentiate these commodity products in the market place.

In order to manufacture the turned parts the company has around 100 machines, some modern CNCs (ie Computer Controlled Machines) and some older, semi-automatic machines. The machines are looked after by skilled direct labour, and they are supported by equally skilled indirect labour, who carry out maintenance functions, etc. It is a mechanical paradise, and the workers take great pride in their work. All told, the total payroll, including administration, sales and management, adds up to 200 people. The turnover is around £5 million. This means that, in a year, turnover per employee is only £25,000. Raw material purchases alone account for 30 per cent or £8,330. Other indirect expenses and overheads take out another 20 per cent or £5,000. In other words, this well-run and efficient business can never afford to pay more than, on average, £12,500 per person in wages.

Example 2 concerns a company that is more typical of manufacturing industry, or of where manufacturing industry is trying to position itself. This company manufactures measuring equipment. The product is still labour-intensive to assemble, but it has certain unique design qualities which prevent it from being seen as a commodity. This allows it to be priced more favourably, but not to the extent that would encourage a competitor to enter the market and undercut. This company also employs 200 people but its annual turnover is around £10 million. In other words, its turnover per employee is £50,000 per annum. The value of the bought-in parts is higher than in Example 1 because they are components and not raw materials, and they amount to around 40 per cent or £20,000 per employee. On top of that the 20 per cent overhead adds another £10,000. This leaves up to £20,000 that could go to paying wages. (In neither example has profit been taken into account.) Clearly this type of company offers a better route to prosperity than does the first example. However, the truth is that neither may be the way forward.

The problem is this. The first company, turning over £25,000 per employee, can turn itself into the second company, turning over £50,000 per employee via two routes. The most desirable way would be to invest in new technology and new working practices, and to thereby double its turnover to £10 million. However, to make this a reality it also has to double its sales. In a commodity market this is not an easy task. Realistically it might take three or four years of sustained effort and additional marketing expenses and it might not be successful. The second way to greater efficiency appeals more to investors interested in short-term measures of success. This is to accept the existing turnover as a ceiling, make half the investment in new technology, dismiss half the workforce

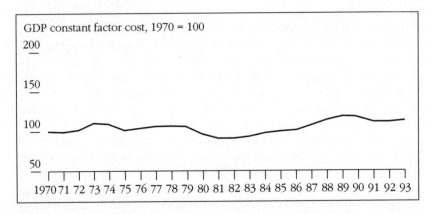

Figure 5.1 *Manufacturing output*

and take the extra profit as dividends. With weak employment protection laws it is easier to dismiss workers, giving only a few weeks' notice, than it is to wait years whilst market share is increased.

The reason why the second company may not offer any more hope is that it is just as likely to be a 400-employee company that downsized to 200 employees, as it is likely to be a new enterprise that has recently grown to offer a genuine 200 new jobs. If Britain, or indeed most western economies, were growing into prosperity instead of downsizing into greater efficiency, then national growth rates would have to be in excess of 6 per cent per annum. This is twice what we are currently achieving and more in keeping with the rapidly expanding Tiger economies of the Far East. Once again the macro figures for Britain speak for themselves.[1] Between 1970 and 1993 total manufacturing output has hardly changed, as demonstrated by figure 5.1, whilst manufacturing employment has fallen from 8.3 million in 1970 to 3.9 million in 1993.

It is genuinely to be hoped that future economic recovery will be based on a revival of the manufacturing sector, but at the same time I fear that this will have little real effect on employment prospects of all those people whose skills predispose them to making their contribution to society through manual dexterity. The point was brought home to me whilst visiting a factory that appeared to be breaking all the records in terms of output per employee. This factory was turning over £20 million and employed just 200 people, in other words, £100,000 per annum per employee. When I asked the manufacturing director how this was achieved, he thought for a moment and then pointed to a line of recently installed robots. These machines cut the raw steel to length and then shaped and drilled it into finished sections ready to be assembled. Each

Table 5.1 *Growth industries*

Company	Revenue per employee $
Packard Bell	925,926
Compaq	716,021
Apple	629,665

Source: *Computer Business Review*, January 1995

Table 5.2 *Older computer industries*

Company	Revenue per employee $
IBM	234,196
HP	253,974
DEC	172,446
ICL	171,167

Source: *Computer Business Review*, January 1995

robot did the work of five men, but that was not the end of it. The robots were run continuously over three shifts, twenty-four hours per day. In other words, they were each doing the work of fifteen people. The wages of the employees were only the same as the norm for the local economy. The benefits of the robotized production were feeding through into competitive advantage and additional profits.

However, we are constantly being told by politicians that 'as a nation' we are all richer than we were ten or twenty years ago, that there are more people in work than there have ever been and that as a consequence we should be 'feeling good'. On the other hand the figures quoted in chapter 1 show that there are more people living in absolute or relative poverty than previously. A split is taking place. If traditional manufacturing is not contributing to the growth in GDP something else must be. One example of a growth industry is still the computer industry, especially where leading-edge technology is being applied, or where substantial amounts of software are involved. Table 5.1 illustrates the point.[2]

Contrast this with the fortunes in table 5.2 of some of the older and more established companies in the industry, whose product lines are often of a more standard type, with some being firmly in the commodity category. DEC and ICL are only just bettering the performance of the robotized engineering company in the example above.

It is the 'headroom' or 'value added' of these higher revenues per employee that allow the payment of wages and salaries well in excess of the national average. Whilst workers in traditional, commodity industry are paid less than the national average, sometimes close to the poverty line, these new knowledge workers can often receive twice, four times or six times the national average. This is where the 'feel good' factor is concentrated. These fortunate workers are not just absorbing the annual increases in GDP that in good years gets up to 3 per cent, they are also absorbing a good deal more as well. This means that substantial numbers of other people displaced by efficiency are suffering real declines in their living standards.

The term 'service industry' is sometimes used to describe both contract cleaning and the provision of information, because neither provides anything tangible in the form of traditionally manufactured goods that can be eaten or worn. However, these are clearly as different as chalk is from cheese. The term is also used to describe the type of economy we are supposed to be moving towards as the millennium approaches. So long as we have images of hi-tech in our minds it constitutes an attractive future. However, in so far as it applies to people providing low-paid personal services, manual services and casual labour it is nothing more than a convenient dumping ground for people that the system is letting down.

6

Which Jobs will Grow and Which Jobs will Go?

It is worth remembering that when agricultural employment collapsed and the move to industrial employment took place, at the start of the industrial revolution in the UK, market forces turned the transition into a nasty and brutal process that took a generation and more to work through, and which at times threatened the very stability of the nation. There was no social security, no safety net to discourage people from learning new skills and taking new jobs. People had to walk for days to find work or starve. If they did find work, then they had to live in the disease-infested slums of the new mill towns.

We are going through a similar transition today. The idea that social upheavals of this magnitude are best managed by a little relocation, a little re-training, and the removal of social security payments that some people think discourage self-sufficiency, is nothing more than a figment of the imagination. Change of this magnitude is painful and disruptive, particularly if its underlying causes are misunderstood. You can't force people into inappropriate employment or non-existent jobs. Even people with the right skills and experience are unable to find work. Ask anyone over the age of fifty how they rate their chances of re-employment should they be made redundant. Just read the job advertisements in the national press that state 'the successful candidate will be in their twenties or early thirties'. Figure 6.1 shows the composition of the labour force according to age. There is sufficient slack in the UK economy to exclude, or downgrade, the contribution of the most experienced 50 per cent of the population.

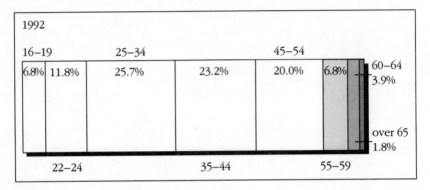

Figure 6.1   *Civilian labour force by age*
Source: Pocket Britain in Figures, 1995

There is a dazzling future out there for any society with the foresight to see it and go for it. It is a future based on technology in which maybe only 10 per cent of the population have to work, in order for the rest of us to have enough of the essentials to be able to live acceptable lives. This ought not to be a revolutionary idea, because it is only a continuation of the trend of the last 200 years. In the agricultural economy nearly everyone had to work at the basics. There was not enough food to go round to allow young people to be absent from the labour force in order to attend school and then university before entering the workforce in their early twenties. There was not enough food, housing, and other essentials to allow large percentages of the workforce to excuse themselves from the basics to pursue employment as nurses, doctors, entertainers, teachers and all the other activities we now consider as work.

Consider how few people today actually provide us with the real basics of life such as food, clothing and shelter. The population of the United Kingdom is around 58 million people. The numbers of workers, part-time and full-time, who provide these basics, are shown in table 6.1.[1] In round figures that means that out of every 100 people just twelve are needed to keep everyone else fed, housed and clothed. This productivity has not happened by accident. It is totally dependent on science and technology, and science and technology is what we are going to get more of in increasing quantities.

The jobs are not all going to disappear overnight. Indeed many new jobs may be created by the new technologies that are being developed.

Table 6.1 *Numbers of workers in primary industries*

Category		Numbers of workers
Agriculture		258,000
Mining		352,000
Manufacturing		3,890,000
Construction		812,000
Power and water		350,000
Transport and communication		1,256,000
	Total	6,918,000
Percentage of population		11.92%

Source: *Pocket Britain in Figures*, 1995

In addition, successful people will have surplus money to spend which could create some trickle-down jobs as well. However, on balance the future will provide fewer jobs and, what is more important, require fewer jobs to be done. The type of jobs that are going to disappear are the ones that have provided the mass employment during the industrial phase of our technological evolution. The type of jobs that will survive from this era are those associated with what are known as the service industries, of which there are two types. Unfortunately one type of service industry job is the traditionally low paid. As more unemployed people chase these remaining employment opportunities they will become even lower paid, if traditional labour market economics are used to gauge their worth.

Martin O'Halloran, the boss of ISS UK which is one of the largest contract cleaning companies in the world, made this point.

> It's easy to knock the idea of a minimum wage when you don't know enough about the damage caused by the lack of it . . .
>
> My company, ISS, employs 135,000 people including 18,000 in the UK, and operates in 32 countries . . .
>
> In the UK, despite efforts by a number of key contractors, the cleaning industry is in a downward wages spiral. In this type of service industry, if you bid for a contract and include decent wage levels, you won't win it . . .
>
> In the UK we are faced with fierce competition based on a pool of cheap labour . . . No one company in isolation can change this . . .
>
> ISS sees the minimum wage as the key to reversing this decline and stopping the erosion of employee benefits.

It would provide a statutory framework for companies to compete on productivity and quality – rather than on how many people they can employ on low wages.

It will help the people we employ in the UK to enjoy a better standard of living. That's something worth fighting for.[2]

These are strong words from someone who knows what he is talking about from first-hand experience. If only others would listen.

The process of job elimination may well not stop at the unskilled and skilled worker. The economist Norman Macrae takes the matter a stage further. He argues that professional people such as doctors, accountants, lawyers and civil servants may soon be made redundant by computer technology, because much of what they do, though clever, is routine and sometimes unnecessary.

Computers are about to cut a swathe through the protected ranks of professional people. . . . Human skills will still be needed, and well paid, but for such truly skilled occupations as gardening and house cleaning.[3]

This refers back to the discussion in chapter 3 concerning Executive Information Systems. Intelligent and highly qualified people have traditionally made their livings by collecting, understanding and interpreting data. It has been a role that only they could fill. Now, however, the computer is evolving into a machine that can do the job more cheaply, more reliably and faster. All it needs is a less skilled person to feed it with the base data. The old professions may well face the sort of downsizing that has been forced on to manufacturing industry.

Management Today put it this way on its front cover: 'No Stability No Security No Careers Welcome to the new deal'.[4] The article goes on to say 'The emerging work paradox is that in a post job world, the only viable long-term career is that of a temp'. It is little wonder that people who would have considered themselves safe in their careers and comfortable with their salary prospects now lack the 'feel good' factor.

Two more articles help to drive home this point. The first appeared in *Barron's*, an influential American magazine written for and read by investors. In this context investors are people who have to look at the world through a mindset of figures. Profits are their guide, and people a disposable asset in the accumulation of those profits. Even the title 'Is a superfluous population becoming an American fixture?' confirms the divergence between the need for profits and the need of the people for jobs.

More than three years into the economic 'recovery' . . . the evidence that America is piling up a surplus workforce is unmistakable.

The anecdotal evidence, of course, has been raining down steadily. Last week alone, job cut announcements included 3,000 at IBM, 6,000 at Kmart, 300 at Cray Research, 590 at Coram Healthcare and 260 at Canandaigua Wine. Today Hughes Aircraft is to have a televised chat with its employees to disclose how much of its workforce will be trimmed, and Digital Equipment will be meeting with its workers to detail how 14,000 of them will be out of a job by next summer. 'Restructuring' and 'downsizing' are most often blamed for the losses and more are on the way. . . .

The disturbing note, however, is that those who are laid off have a significantly smaller chance than their parents did of finding a new job, or at least finding one quickly: Not only has the unemployment rate remained stubbornly above 6 per cent, but it's likely to start rising again as the Fed keeps ratcheting up interest rates. A generation ago, full employment meant a jobless rate of 4 per cent; now . . . the threshold has ballooned to 6.5 per cent. The social policy implications of that number are enormous, if largely ignored, although Fed Vice Chairman Alan Blinder caused a ruckus last week by reaffirming his belief that the central bank should consider the unemployment rate when fiddling with interest rates. Meanwhile, one glimmer of a silver lining is provided by the temporary-help industry . . .[5]

The second article appeared in the *Washington Post* summarizing a speech by Labour Secretary Robert B. Reich.

Reich posed the question, 'Is the cost of being competitive too high if it means a lower standard of living for middle-class Americans?' The point he was making was that economic growth that did not result in rising living standards for most people was of questionable value.

One problem Reich identified was the eight million unemployed people and another four million people who were working part-time but who wanted full-time jobs. All this when Wall Street was worrying about inflationary pressure as a result of tight labour markets for workers with higher skill levels.

This growing gap between skilled and less-skilled workers is causing concern in government departments. At the beginning of the 1980s a white male college graduate earned 49 per cent more than a colleague with only a high school diploma, yet they both enjoyed middle-class status. Today the earnings differential has widened to over 80 per cent, and many are no longer able to enjoy a middle-class lifestyle. As Reich is quoted as saying:

The cold war ended dramatically. We watched it on CNN . . . But America's middle class crumbled quietly . . . We watched it happen day by day but somehow we never saw it. And now are confront its consequences.

We can't all be computer programmers or rocket scientists. The human race is comprised of people of mixed abilities and this diversity should be a source of strength. Adam Smith in the Wealth of Nations said:

> The patrimony of a poor man lies in the strength and dexterity of his hands; and to hinder him from employing this . . . is a plain violation of this most sacred property.

People with just their labour to sell have only been able to escape from the trap of low wages by linking their skills to machinery, and thereby boosting their productivity and their earning capacity. If the machines become clever enough to look after themselves then the human component is redundant, and with it the relatively high wages that have been available to this section of the population, and indeed to other sectors too. We are moving towards a new type of economy, one based on knowledge, but not just the processing of knowledge. Instead of machines being the method of leveraging up wages in the future, knowledge will be the means by which people escape from the trap of low pay. However, this route will only be available to the section of the population mentally equipped to take advantage of this development. The dextrous intelligence of the manual worker and the predictable intelligence of many professionals will not be suited to this opportunity. Instead it will be the preserve of those people who can control, manipulate and, in particular, creatively use this knowledge.

Personal services are often advanced as the way employment will evolve, but our attitudes towards personal services are, in part, responsible for the low esteem in which they are held and therefore the low pay that they command. To serve someone else has traditionally put the servant in an inferior position. The employers dump on to someone else all the jobs they do not want to do, or feel are beneath their status. Inferior people are worth less than superior people. How much less can depend upon the superiority complex of the employer. In class-based societies that sense of superiority can be overwhelming and condemn the lower orders of society to the meanest of existences.

Another problem with the master/servant attitude towards the creation of employment is that it links employment opportunities to the personal earning power of the master. As recently as sixty years ago, just before the Second World War, live-in domestic work was a major source of employment. A professional man's family might have had in its employment two or three maids, a chauffeur and a gardener. If the master of the house allocated 20 per cent of his income to paying the domestics their wages, then arithmetic dictates that if they were all paid the same, they would each earn only 4 per cent of what the master earned, an earnings differential of twenty-five times. Sometimes the younger domestics received no pay, just their keep. The creation of employment through domestic service therefore implies the creation of very large differences in the distribution of wealth within a society and the maintenance of those differentials. The very rich employ the very poor. It is also limited to the number of people who can afford to keep servants.

Catering, cleaning, gardening, sweeping, waiting on, hair cutting, laundry, baby minding are all the things that rich people could do for themselves, but would have had done for them by personal servants. They are still characterized by very low rates of pay, even though these activities are seldom provided by 'in-house' labour any more. Fast-food restaurants, office cleaning, hospital catering, retail service, child care and the care of elderly people, etc. provide the numerical bulk of the employment opportunities in the emerging service economy. Unfortunately, as they are remunerated at present, they do not provide the basis of a high wage economy that can deliver improving standards of living to the majority of the population in the future. Wealth can afford to ignore this fact because it will always have access to the best, provided by its own ring-fenced micro-economy. However, the majority of the population depend for their own standards of living on the disposable income of their neighbours. If a significant sector of the economy is to be based on low pay, this will drag down the living standards of all those who depend upon selling goods and services to that sector of the population.

There can be no such thing as a smooth transition between two economic states, when the change is as fundamental and as rapid as the one that is now taking place. It is not a gradual move but a major discontinuity spread over a considerable period of time. Those sections of the population that are displaced set in motion a downwards spiral of economic disinvestment. Their ability to express their needs in the market place through the medium of money declines. Falling demand deters business people from making investments and leads to the closure of existing enterprises. This gives the spiral a further downward twist and so it goes on. The old industrial centres of the North of England and the rust belt towns of North America are ample testament to this. Keynes recognized the process and christened it the Demand Deficit. Once it sets in motion, there is only one organization capable of mitigating its worst effects, and that is the state. If the jobs are not there, and at decent levels of wages, then there is no way the numbers of people displaced can climb back into the formal economy. Jobs that pay low, or poverty-line wages, are no more than a holding operation, slowing or stabilizing the rate of decline.

Once again our attitudes hold one of the keys to a more prosperous future. Our attitudes define the possibilities open to us. Can we adjust our ways of thinking so that we see personal service in a new light? Can we pay others more so that in turn they can buy more from us? We look up to the man dressed in a white overall and call him doctor and pay him well. We look down on the man dressed in a brown overall and call him a labourer and pay him badly. However, the richer they both are, the richer we all are. The poorer either is, the poorer we all are. We can set up either a virtuous or a vicious spiral in which the world becomes either richer or poorer.

Assuming that we are able to adjust and reward all service jobs generously, there is still another obstacle to overcome. This obstacle is one of quantity. Are there enough service industry jobs to go round, to mop up the unemployment created by the demise of traditional industrial employment? Will there be enough hierarchies of wealth and activity within which the majority of the population will be able to find employment?

Labour-saving devices are being invented that will perform the work previously done by domestic labour. The washing machine is a prime example. There is hardly a house that does not have one. This means that we cannot survive by taking in each other's dirty washing. Prepared convenience foods mean that the jobs of cooks and maids are also redundant. There is not much point in looking for growth in service industry employment in the area of domestic services. Nor is there much point in looking to the speculative aspects of 'service' economy activity to provide real long-term jobs.

The 1980s saw a frenzy of economic activity which many people mistook for the arrival of a new age. In Britain the Chancellor of the Exchequer pronounced that manufacturing industry was no longer important and that service industries had taken over. People were finding employment as stockbrokers, estate agents, bank employees, financial advisers and in all manner of other non-productive activities. This may seem a little harsh, but an economy only needs a few such services to support the orderly transfer of existing assets between citizens. When such activities start to drive the economy what they are really doing is just churning it up. People may move house two or three times in a lifetime. If they suddenly start buying and selling houses speculatively to make money, then a speculative boom is under way, which inevitably will come to an end, and with it the employment that it temporarily created. It might be possible to run an economy in the future on speculative buying and selling, if a way could be found of preventing asset values from falling, but that has not yet happened. Constant speculation is impossible, and prices will always lapse back to what society feels comfortable with.

Jobs might be created in the provision of true personal services that are unlikely to be replaced by machines for the foreseeable future, but this is a very difficult area. The British, for example, are a reserved race when it comes to these matters. What new personal services could we all start to use that would generate employment on a sustainable and well-paid basis? If we all went for a haircut and manicure or a massage every week, tens of thousands of jobs would be created in those trades. If we all saw a personal psychiatrist once a week there would be employment opportunities there. If we all stopped doing DIY jobs ourselves, and employed trades people, then tens of thousands of jobs would be created for people whose intelligence finds its expression through manual skills. A society based on this type of service could work if we could accept these things into our culture and value them enough to pay well for them.

The idea of paying a waiter in a hotel as much as we pay a chief accountant in an international corporation may seem a ridiculous idea now, and be offensive to the accountant, but it may be an important way to keep the system going in the future by keeping the money going round. The work the waiter does is as physically demanding as the work that the accountant does is mentally demanding. The accountant is paid more because there are supposedly fewer people able to do his type of work than there are people who can serve at table. Professional people in general have also been clever enough to bolster their positions by restricting entry to their professions except through formal competitive examinations. However, the accountant is only where he is in the salary league because other people earn enough money for him to count. If the traditional well-paid manual jobs in the economy go away, then they will take with them the careers of many professional people in the service economy, such as lawyers, dentists, estate agents, stockbrokers and of course our accountant. It is in everyone's interests to value all services highly enough, so that they can be rewarded well enough, because we are all part of the same system. Our attitudes need to adapt to this simple fact, and our ego does too.

Another more promising area of service industry employment is in the leisure industry sector. This area has been expanding year on year. It covers everything from health clubs to hotels. It depends for its future growth on two things. These are, that there is a continuing growth in free time, and a continuing growth in disposable income to spend in that free time. In other words, we have to be paid more and we have to work less in order to make a leisure-based economy work. A leisure economy

based on the enforced leisure of unemployment or low wages is a contradiction in terms. An economy based around the wealth of the few is
a luxury economy, not a leisure economy.

If we are serious about creating a leisure-based economy, then we
have to start to take seriously the idea of further reducing working hours,
as a means of sharing out both the work and the leisure, whilst at the
same time maintaining everyone's current level of wages and salaries.
This could be achieved over a number of years if done in phase with the
rapid increases in productivity that are taking place. Of course this will
make individual firms uncompetitive if all companies are not required
to do it. However, if all companies are required to do it then there is no
problem as everyone faces the same cost structure. Furthermore, there is
one huge bonus to be had from this arrangement. A new source of
demand will be created as people are drawn back into the waged economy. Demand against which companies can invest. Demand which will
set in motion a virtuous spiral of prosperity and individual financial independence which, in turn, will reduce the need for the state to spend
so much on welfare.

I suspect that people locked into a competitive mindset will have a
problem with this idea. Essentially the competitive mindset is only looking
at winning and holding on to the winnings. It is not looking at re-defining
the rules so that there are more winners. However, what sort of a mess
would our economy be in today if we still had the rates of pay of the
early industrial revolution days? What would our quality of life be like if
we still had the sixty-five-hour or more working week of those times?
Certainly any company that could get away with such conditions would
have an enormous competitive advantage, but it is up to people with
more sense to point to the larger picture and prevent such things from
happening.

However, if we are not yet ready to radically re-define the working
week we must still ask where are the new, well-paid, service industry
jobs going to come from, that will give employment to the majority of the
population in the future?

When we talk about work we automatically think first about paid
employment in the formal economy. However, this is only a fraction of
the work that gets done in the world today. Most work is done within
families or communities and it is done for no wages. What is the cost of
giving birth to a healthy baby? What is the value of the work any mother
does every day looking after the children and tidying the house? What
is the value of a son or daughter looking after elderly parents in their declining years? If we are so hooked on only paying wages for work done
then there is massive scope for re-defining what we mean by work. If

mothers were paid a wage for bringing up children there would never be an unemployment problem. It would also mark the end of a male-dominated society and world. Is this something that the men could accept? The idea of young, single women deliberately becoming pregnant in order to get on to welfare is a highly controversial and emotive subject.

Peter Drucker seems to take the view that it is a problem to be managed.

> The knowledge society is a society in which many more people than ever can be successful. But it is therefore, by definition, a society in which many more people than ever can fail, or at least come in second . . . The right answer to the question Who takes care of the social challenges of the knowledge society? is . . . a separate and new social sector . . . The knowledge society has to be a society of three sectors: a public sector of government, a private sector of business and a social sector . . . Through the social sector a modern developed society can again create responsible and achieving citizenship, and can again give individuals . . . a sphere in which they can make a difference in society and recreate community.[7]

These are excellent sentiments with which I concur, but again one question remains open. Where in traditional market-oriented economics exist the practical mechanisms for financing this new social sector, so that it is not just a drain on society's money, but a powerful source of legitimate demand, driving the evolution of our increasingly automated economy?

The successful people referred to above will probably fall into six categories. There is a seventh category, that of established wealth. However, this category is a fixture of the socio-economic scene and so does not constitute anything new.

Firstly, there will be those people who can invent new technologies and find uses for them. The overall size of this opportunity will depend upon how much investment is put into research and development by large commercial organizations. It will also depend upon how effort is directed. If it is directed narrowly only at areas where there is monetary demand and a chance at profitable payback, instead of a wider remit covering society's needs, then it will fail to mobilize all of our potential.

Secondly, there will be a need for people who can supervise the new technologies. Ultimately the technologies will become self-contained and not require human intervention, but whilst they are being introduced they will require supervision, until we understand the full implications of their introduction and come to trust their safety and security.

Thirdly, there will be a need for technicians who can make the new technologies work in the way that they are intended to work. As with the second category above, it will be people who carry out the implementations in the early days.

Fourthly, there will be a need for experts to explain to us the new technologies and how we should use them. There will also be a requirement for experts to sort out the problems and disputes that will inevitably arise over the use, or misuse, of the new technologies.

Fifthly, there will be a need for people to sell and distribute the output of the new technologies to those people who can afford to pay for such goods and services.

Sixthly, there will be a requirement for security, to insulate the beneficiaries of this new technology from the potentially hostile attentions of the sections of society not benefiting from these developments.

Business Week portrays the position as shown in figure 6.2.[8] The chart shows a growth in the less numerous top jobs, a growth in the more numerous very low-paid jobs, and a collapse in the reasonably paid jobs that have swelled the ranks of the middle classes in recent decades.

Another approach taken by other commentators is to re-define work. For example Charles Handy, in his book *The Empty Raincoat*, speculates that we will have to react to the new technology by having a portfolio of skills that will equip us for many different careers throughout our working lives. In other words the successful workers of the future will have to be adaptable, resourceful, and above all re-trainable so that they can adjust to the changing job patterns of new technology. What is more they will probably only find employment for 50,000 hours instead of the current working lifetime of 100,000 hours.[9] Once again this raises the question of how current living standards will be maintained or pensions funded.

William Bridges, author of *Jobshift* and several other books and articles, saw this type of change coming in the early 1980s. Working with companies in the computer industry, he noticed that employees did not have jobs so much as a series of assignments, which could be many and varied. Today he believes that the concept of a job that offers a secure career structure is obsolete. He predicts that, looking back in twenty-five years' time, we will see our present chase to create jobs as fighting over the deck chairs on the *Titanic*.

An Editorial in the *Calgary Sun* points out the ultimate irony.

> There is something agonisingly ironic about the scenario of Canada Employment Centre workers lining up on the other side of the counter.
>
> Some 100 employees in Calgary and thousands more across the country will lose their jobs in the next few years as they are replaced by machines dispensing advice and information to the unemployed on how to find jobs.
>
> This conjures up an image that perfectly epitomizes the technological and political upheaval of the '90s. Not even workers in the growth industry of unemployment are secure in their positions.[10]

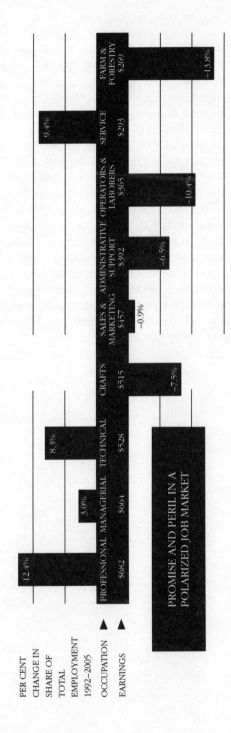

Figure 6.2 *Promise and peril in a polarized job market*

Source: US Bureau of Labor Statistics, occupational forecast for the year 2005. Reprinted from 17 October, 1994 issue of *Business Week* by special permission, © 1994 by The McGraw-Hill Companies.

This is the nub of the problem. In answer to the question posed in the title of this chapter, we probably have very little control over the destruction of specific jobs by new technology. We probably have some control over the volume of new jobs that technology will create, if we invest to create well-paid jobs, and thereby start a virtuous spiral. What we have to worry about is how all the people, probably the majority, who are displaced by this process, can be reintegrated into society as assets and not liabilities. There simply will not be enough well-paid jobs to go round if it is left to the market. We can increase the number of well-paid jobs at the margins by re-evaluating our attitudes to work based on personal services and traditional crafts. However this will not be enough. What is important is how we react to the challenge. Do we manage it as a problem, and therefore a cost, to be minimized by marginalizing into poverty those people who cannot adapt or are not needed, or do we try to find radical new opportunities to fit the new circumstances?

The twentieth century started with a working week of sixty-five hours. Are we prepared to see the twenty-first century start with a working week of thirty hours, to bring back into line the amount of labour now required to operate our highly automated capital base?

7

Can We Rely on the Enterprise Culture and the Small Business to Solve our Problems?

The British economy has been downsizing in line with technology. There are now only approximately 5,000 commercial organizations in the UK that employ more than 400 people. Some of these companies are very large with thousands of employees, but overall the days of the mass employer seem to be drawing to a close. Manufacturing industry is a typical example of this. In 1983 there were 157,734 production sites in the UK, some very small, employing 6.94 million people.[1] In 1993 the total number of sites was roughly the same at 161,791, but they employed only 3.89 million people. Over this same period total output has remained roughly constant[2] so it has been a case, not of growth, but of fewer people making the same amount.

In general terms the shape of the British economy is shown in table 7.1. The idea that all the UK's employment problems could be solved by small companies taking on one or two additional workers each has a convenient political appeal to it, but it overlooks an important fact. There are probably already too many small companies in the UK economy and not enough medium and large companies. It should be a warning to everyone to see just how few companies there are with significant turnovers. Just look at manufacturing with only 4,024 sites turning over more than £10 million. Is that a basis on which an advanced economy can take on global competition and win?

The figure of £10 million in turnover is important. Most of the large multinational corporations and conglomerates are formed of units of this size or greater. If an entrepreneur manages to grow a company to this size, then he or she will probably be able to 'cash out' by selling the

Table 7.1 United Kingdom – number and percentage of legal units in 1993 VAT trade classification by turnover sizeband

	Turnover size (£ thousand)[b,c]											
	1–34		35–49		50–99		100–249		250–499		500–999	
Agriculture, forestry and fishing	66,471	41%	16,868	10%	32,489	20%	30,858	19%	9,864	6%	3,707	2%
Production	27,056	17%	12,974	8%	25,765	16%	33,424	21%	19,808	13%	14,139	9%
Mining and quarrying and public utilities[a]	218	14%	80	5%	167	11%	248	16%	175	11%	165	11%
Manufacturing[a]	26,838	17%	12,894	8%	25,598	16%	33,176	21%	19,633	13%	13,974	9%
Construction	55,367	26%	31,105	15%	46,979	22%	41,043	19%	17,988	8%	10,558	5%
Transport industries	15,525	22%	11,022	16%	14,948	21%	11,398	16%	6,212	9%	4,606	7%
Road transport and transport services	14,827	22%	10,814	16%	14,637	22%	11,039	17%	5,954	9%	4,357	7%
Other transport	698	24%	208	7%	311	11%	359	12%	258	9%	249	8%
Postal services and telecommunications	449	27%	210	13%	267	16%	272	17%	134	8%	117	7%
Wholesaling and dealing	25,980	19%	10,653	8%	18,648	13%	24,814	18%	17,301	12%	15,348	11%
Retailing	20,833	9%	22,273	9%	62,069	26%	81,614	35%	30,931	13%	11,937	5%
Finance, property and professional services	50,356	29%	26,508	15%	34,827	20%	27,543	16%	13,141	8%	8,065	5%
Catering	6,109	5%	12,677	11%	37,303	31%	45,238	38%	11,568	10%	3,774	3%
Motor trades	9,474	12%	7,902	10%	14,578	19%	16,560	22%	9,459	12%	7,180	9%
Business services and central offices	39,855	30%	22,296	17%	27,134	20%	19,137	14%	8,885	7%	6,221	5%
All other services	38,986	29%	22,770	17%	31,899	24%	23,835	18%	8,953	7%	4,665	3%
Total	356,461	22%	197,258	12%	346,906	21%	355,736	22%	154,244	10%	90,317	6%

Turnover size (£ thousand)

	1,000–1,999		2,000–4,999		5,000–9,999		10,000 and over		Total
Agriculture, forestry and fishing	1,243	1%	481	0%	118	0%	79	0%	162,178
Production	9,332	6%	7,357	5%	3,179	2%	4,212	3%	157,246
Mining and quarrying and public utilities[a]	124	8%	127	8%	79	5%	188	12%	1,571
Manufacturing	9,208	6%	7,230	5%	3,100	2%	4,024	3%	155,675
Construction	5,384	3%	3,133	1%	985	0%	969	0%	213,511
Transport industries	2,713	4%	1,828	3%	647	1%	830	1%	69,729
Road transport and transport services	2,486	4%	1,601	2%	515	1%	559	1%	66,789
Other transport	227	8%	227	8%	132	4%	271	9%	2,940
Postal services and telecommunications	73	4%	54	3%	29	2%	39	2%	1,644
Wholesaling and dealing	11,396	8%	8,943	6%	3,277	2%	3,010	2%	139,370
Retailing	4,151	2%	1,675	1%	444	0%	597	0%	236,524
Finance, property and professional services	4,559	3%	3,224	2%	1,505	1%	3,000	2%	172,728
Catering	1,176	1%	562	0%	144	0%	142	0%	118,693
Motor trades	4,990	7%	3,579	5%	1,247	2%	914	1%	75,883
Business services and central offices	3,440	3%	2,725	2%	1,234	1%	1,934	1%	132,861
All other services	1,785	1%	1,111	1%	423	0%	576	0%	135,003
Total	50,242	3%	34,672	2%	13,232	1%	16,302	1%	1,615,370

[a] The definition of manufacturing, mining and quarrying and public utilities is aligned to SIC (1968).

[b] Turnover relates mainly to a 12-month period ending in Spring 1992.

[c] Excludes 56,241 units with zero turnover.

Source: *Size Analysis of United Kingdom Business 1993*. Reproduced by the permission of the Controller of HMSO and the Central Statistical Office.

Table 7.2 *Manufacturing companies, employment*

People	1–19	20–49	50–99	100–199	200+
Number of firms	111,370	16,688	7,229	4,504	4,071

Source: Size Analysis of United Kingdom Businesses 1993

business to a larger concern or by 'floating' the business on the stock exchange. At this turnover the business will have the potential to show a 10 per cent profit of £1 million. It will have the resources to fund some research and development. It will have the resources to afford overseas representation. Above all, if it receives additional investment, it will have the potential to grow into an even more substantial enterprise. If it is given the investment and stability and it does grow further then it could, over a period of years, turn into a world beater. On the other hand, if it is starved of investment and milked like a 'cash cow', or if it is bought and sold like an inconsequential object, then it will fade and ultimately fail.

Small companies are nice to have around. They do provide employment but they lack the resources of their larger brethren. Indeed they usually survive by taking in subcontract work from larger companies. In recession or faced with severe competition, they fail at a faster rate than do the larger concerns. Consequently, the employment that they offer tends to be less secure, wages tend to be lower and fringe benefits, such as pension arrangements, are less comprehensive. They often tend to be less ambitious, existing to provide their owners with a higher quality of life than they might otherwise enjoy working in larger, more pressurized, companies. However the fight for survival that many small firms face gives rise to its own form of stress.

From the figures shown in table 7.1 there are 4,024 manufacturing companies in the UK turning over £10,000,000 or more per annum. This also corresponds to companies employing more than 200 people, already referred to in Chapter 5. The official figures are shown in table 7.2. If the UK, or any other western economy, is going to survive as a major industrial power, there will have to be more emphasis on 'growing' companies that can compete internationally and not just act as sponges to suck up local unemployment. Small companies that stay small are not the answer. Technology may keep reducing the payrolls of the larger companies but at least the larger companies have access to resources, particularly cash, and this is crucial in the fight for survival.

Companies can be 'grown' through two routes. The first is by large organizations investing in new ideas. This is the surest way of ensuring

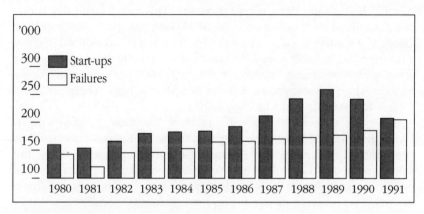

Figure 7.1 *Business start-ups and failures*
Source: Pocket Britain in Figures, 1995

success. Everything that a new venture needs can be provided and with this kind of help most good ideas will succeed. However, not all good ideas are recognized by large companies, who may be a little too content with the success of their present portfolios of products. Additionally, in companies which have to watch their dividends and share prices, the will to invest in new ventures with the extra risk involved may just not be there.

The second route to 'growing' new companies is through entrepre-neurial start-ups. Entrepreneurs are the folk heroes of the free enterprise system. Capitalism based on individual achievement. An assortment of enterprising individuals riding to the rescue of a moribund economy. This is the hard way, because the fledgling company can go bust whilst it is developing, and many do. Bank managers and other professionals will tell you that up to 50 per cent of new start-up companies go out of business within the first two years. Of the rest many will remain small, some because they have to, and others because their owners want them to. After five years maybe only one in 100 will have grown to be turning over £5 million and employing 100 people. If a society wants to grow its industrial base by this method and thereby cure its unemployment prob-lems, then it has to accept that success only comes about with lots of failure. Figures for start-ups and failures are given in figure 7.1.

Efficiency is growing in the British economy at 3 per cent per annum. With a working population of 25 million this means that up to 750,000 people are being displaced each year and have to find new jobs. If all these people were to find work in growing companies of £5 million turnover, then each year we would have to see 7,500 of these companies coming through the process and surviving. This could mean that if one in ten survived then out of an original 75,000 start-ups 67,500 will have failed. If the success ratio is one in 100, then out of an original 750,000 a massive 742,500 will have failed or stayed small. Business start-ups are actually running at only around 200,000 to 250,000 per year, which could explain why unemployment remains persistently high. There could be far too few start-ups and too few failures.

However, whatever the true figure is, if this route to prosperity is taken, then we will have to be prepared to encourage risk-taking and be very tolerant of failure. If we punish the entrepreneurs for trying but failing, in the end they will give up trying. When failure happens innocent people get hurt. Wages go unpaid, creditors lose their money, but this is the price we all have to pay for an entrepreneurial society.

As usual, it is easier to talk about encouraging an entrepreneurial society than paying for one to happen. In the UK the venture capital industry provides a surprisingly small amount of money to back business start-ups. Figures from the British Venture Capital Association show that significant amounts of funding were provided to only a very few companies. The peak year was 1989, when just over 500 start-up companies received £215 million between them. This is peanuts when one established public company can invest several times this amount in one project alone. In 1994 the picture looked far bleaker. Only 190 start-up companies were backed to the tune of £76 million. Commercial banks still provide the largest source of funding for private companies, usually through the provision of overdrafts and loans. However, they also require personal guarantees from the entrepreneur that discourage all but the bravest. In the event that these guarantees are called, the individuals concerned can lose everything, including their houses and thereby become a charge on the state. Rich, private individuals will often take risks with start-ups but, because these are private arrangements, there are no figures to show their contribution.

An entrepreneurial society can be a society in turmoil in more ways than that just mentioned above. When entrepreneurs are operating in new territory they can be trailblazers. However, when they are operating in territory occupied by established enterprises, their activities can be destructive to those enterprises. Certainly there are times when tired organizations need shaking up, but there are as many times when the companies are well managed and just need leaving alone to continue making steady, not spectacular, progress. The stock market raiders of the 1980s in the USA and the UK did untold damage to companies that did not need their attentions, or the mountains of debt that their strategies brought with them. This was not renewal by creative destruction as

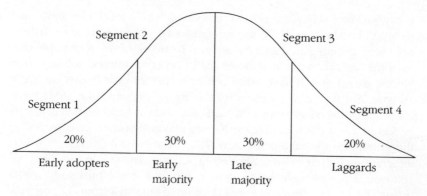

Figure 7.2 *Buying styles by market segment*

envisioned by economic theory, it was competitive destruction driven by individual greed.

Entrepreneurs are important in a free market economy, but their role can be over-emphasized. Entrepreneurs do kick-start businesses. They do see opportunities that others fail to spot or would prefer not to see. However, having created a company by strength of personality and a hands-on approach, there comes a time when they should hand over to professional managers who possess business skills of a different sort. Too many entrepreneurs fail to recognize their limitations and drive successful companies back into the ground chasing the next big idea. Established businesses need to be professionally run. They need a steady hand and, as far as possible, a steady business environment.

Big business too can be beguiled by the entrepreneurial myth. Anyone familiar with sales and marketing will recognize the market profile shown in figure 7.2 and described by Geoffrey Moore.[3] Entrepreneurs and new products operate in the first segment. Entrepreneurs sell to 'early adopters' and 'early adopters' are predisposed to buy new products. Early adopters like new products. An early adopter will buy the first microwave cooker, the first electric car, the first hi-tech golf club, be the first user of a new software package, and he or she will pay a premium for the privilege. The entrepreneur will earn his above-average profits from this sector of the market, which is generally judged to be about 20 per cent of the total market potential. In business early adopters will purchase new, relatively untried products because they think that, with them, they will gain a competitive edge over the competition. This is why they are also willing to pay a premium price for the privilege.

The 'early majority' are reassured by the fact that the early adopters have taken the risk of trying out the new product, but they are not that easily satisfied. They are not so impressed with spectacular individual technical breakthroughs. To the early majority, products are not safe bets until they are integrated into the wider scheme of things. A buyer of cars for a fleet rental company may see the benefits of running pollution-free electric cars, but will have other concerns that will not bother the early adopter. Are the electric cars as reliable as the present vehicles? Is there a network of service centres? What is the second-hand market likely to be for the used electric vehicles? If early majority buyers are considering the purchase of revolutionary new software they will consider if it will integrate with their existing systems. They will realize that one piece of software is not enough, on its own, to run their entire business, and so they will wait until the supplier has developed links to a family of products that in total offer a more comprehensive solution. To these buyers the competitive advantage has to be weighed against any possible disruption or discontinuity that might be caused. They may still be willing to pay a fair price for the product, but they expect more. This in turn requires the entrepreneur supplier to reinvest more of the profits into creating a broader and more stable product. At this stage the entrepreneur may begin to lose interest, because the original excitement of being at the leading edge is starting to fade and the profit margins are starting to be squeezed.

This is a crucial make or break phase for a product. This segment of the market represents around 30 per cent of the total. If the incumbent suppliers can be successfully challenged and the market conquered (an expensive exercise) then this is where the bulk of the profits are in volume terms, not percentage terms.

The 'late majority' are not really interested in new technology. They already have something in place that works and which they understand and feel comfortable with. If they are going to invest in something new, then it is because what they already have has reached the end of its working life and cannot be repaired any more. Indeed the thought of all the disruption and of having to learn a new skill is something they could do without. They certainly will not be the first to try something new. They will look around the industry and see what everyone else is using because that represents the safest bet. They will probably end up purchasing the market leader product. Furthermore they will expect to get it at a cheaper price. After all, the product will have been in the market place for some time now and all its development costs will have been written off. This is the point at which the entrepreneur becomes decidedly uninterested and returns to the starting point with another new idea. Both the good profits and the excitement appear to have deserted the product. However, this segment of the market is another 30 per cent of the total. It can be very easy for the market leaders to sell into, and it represents a continuing, if unspectacular, profit opportunity.

The 'laggards' are those people who really do not see the need for any change whatsoever. Pencil and paper are good enough writing implements so why should anyone want to invent a computerized word processor to do the job? Steam trains got passengers from A to B so why are electric trains necessary? Traditional ways are always better than new ideas. These people are the counterbalance to the early adopters and represent the last 20 per cent of the market. However, before we poke fun at these people we should realize that at different times we each can occupy all of the market segments. Some members of the early majority at work may be the first to buy a hi-tech golf club, because they are passionate about winning at golf. The same person may be a laggard when it comes to taking out insurance or pension policies. They might represent something that they do not understand, and so they have stuck with the same company and the same policies ever since their first paycheque.

So how does this relate to company behaviour? The answer is that if the bosses of companies see themselves as too much the charismatic entrepreneur and not enough the steady manager, then they will turn their backs on most of the market that could be theirs. This behaviour can be reinforced by the judgement of the stock markets. In the USA and the UK, investors in the stock markets are always looking for the best performers, those companies that turn in spectacular profits. Unfortunately, spectacular profits are usually only available to entrepreneurial companies selling to the early adopter phase of the market. If a company selling to the early or late majority, is turning in spectacular profits, then it is probably because it is skimping on the investment necessary to keep it in position in those market segments. Spectacular percentage profits are not usually available in the early or late majority market segments. By the time a product reaches the late majority it is pretty much a commodity, commanding commodity prices. With relentless competition from low-cost producers and the sort of efficiency measures discussed in chapter 5, year-on-year price reductions may be its only future.

How often do we hear the lament 'invented here, manufactured elsewhere'? The point is that new inventions are often manufactured first in the USA or the UK, but when the early adopters have been sold to and the spectacular profits have left the products, or the patent rights have expired, then the originating companies lose the will to continue the production with a different set of profit expectations. They are off chasing the next big idea to impress the stock exchange and their shareholders. But at this stage the products have only penetrated 20 per cent of the market. Japan and other Far Eastern countries made their industrial entries on to the world stage with copycat products, and by manufacturing those things that western nations were not prepared to put effort into. The biggest players in commercial ship building are now mainly located in the Far East. Japan leads in the manufacture of electronics. They have also reshaped the world's automobile manufacturing industries. The list of high-volume, low-profit products that they now dominate is endless.

The point that profit-chasing western business has missed is a simple one. The power base that the low-profit, somewhat dull, 60 per cent of the market offers, is a power base from which the high profit 20 per cent of the market can be challenged and won. When this happens the losing economy is left with even less to offer its population by way of employment.

Another point that now seems to be lost on western politicians wedded to extreme free-market thinking is that of a 'critical mass of business activity'. This oversight may be explained by the fact that they have not yet fully appreciated the importance of the increasing amount of economic activity that is under the domination of multinational companies. Multinationals demand the right to locate and relocate as their profits dictate, but they also have the economic resources to make things happen wherever they settle. However, the budding entrepreneur needs the support of a friendly environment.

Establishing new enterprises is made significantly more easy if a basic infrastructure is in place. This can be the obvious, such as roads, telecommunications, etc., but the most effective infrastructure is a critical mass of business concentration. A single factory has it all to do for itself, if it does not have the resources of an international corporation behind it, but once enough companies have set up in an area, the important support networks can come into being. Educational colleges will find it worthwhile to run courses, training agencies will run skills training, business clubs will share information and provide support in problem solving. Banks will develop an understanding of how local industries function and be more inclined to lend capital to the business community. In total, a reserve of local expertise develops that start-up ventures can call on. This phenomenon happened in Lancashire between 1860 and 1914 with the cotton textile industry based around Manchester as its commercial hub. Satellite manufacturing towns such as Ashton, Rochdale, Oldham, Bury, Bolton, Stockport and many others could each boast several hundred textile mills apiece. These mills needed servicing with all manner of machinery and supplies. The Platts textile machinery factory in Oldham had seventeen thousand workers on the one site. Not only were there business opportunities to be had in the primary activity of producing cotton textiles, there were as many, or more, to be had in servicing those firms. Start-up businesses were more likely to succeed than fail in these optimistic conditions, and it is reputed that there were more millionaires living in these few square miles than anywhere else on the planet.

From being a windswept agricultural county with heavy clay soils fit only for growing potatoes, Lancashire grew to be the world's premier textile-manufacturing area. The supporting population that was encouraged into existence in a belt of land less than 100 miles long, bounded by the port of Liverpool in the west and the Yorkshire cities of Leeds and Bradford in the east, numbers over 15 million people. For over fifty years between 1860 and 1914 a spiral of prosperity, interrupted at times, existed that fed on itself. The First World War marked the end of this success story. There are authenticated stories of working-class men wearing £5 notes (a month's wages for some) in their hatbands to show off their prosperity. Today's equivalent might be £500. Similar extravagant behaviour has been witnessed during the 1980s amongst dealers in the financial markets. In fact the cotton workers sporting the £5 notes may well have been dealing on the side in the shares of the local mills. So great was the optimism that part-paid shares were offered locally to finance the building of many of the mills.

Since the 1920s the story of the Lancashire textile industry has been one of steady decline. Many people who bought in late, into the false boom that followed the end of the First World War, lost their money and more, if they had over-extended themselves with part-paid shares. The war gave producers in the Pacific time to build up capacity, which broke the Lancashire monopoly. The decline may have been inevitable, but the real failure is that nothing as substantial as the textile industry has been put in place to maintain the prosperity of the region. Lancashire always believed in free trade, but when the free market moved on, 15 million people had to stay where they were and do the best that they could. Efforts at diversification have been made and the industrial base of the area is more varied, but somehow it's just not been enough to counteract the massive disinvestment in textiles. Unemployment is high and wages are low. The port of Liverpool has suffered the most, as it depends upon the volume of activity in its hinterland. Liverpool is now officially one of the poorest and most deprived areas in the European Community, and receives special grant aid as a result. The economic policies promoted by the British government during the 1980s served only to further disadvantage the local economy.

A similar phenomenon has occurred in California in Silicon Valley, where everything to do with computers is to hand within this one sprawling location. This includes the millionaires, who have succeeded once and understand the business, and who are willing to risk some of their cash funding new start-ups. Silicon Valley has not yet reached its peak, but then it has not yet been going for fifty years.

When enterprise and enterprises start to desert an area and the critical mass is lost the decline can become terminal. A multinational company may have good reason to shift production to a low-wage country, but in so doing it wounds the economy that it is deserting. If enough companies desert the area then the spiral of prosperity can be reversed. If you are not going forwards then you are going to go backwards. The option to stand still does not exist. One company, judged by its balance sheet performance, may not be profitable enough to satisfy profit-maximizing accountants. However, that company does not exist in isolation. It has suppliers and its purchases may be what makes those suppliers profitable, and so on down the whole supply chain.

Unfortunately, that view of the overall situation is of no concern to the lead company, nor to its suppliers who also account for their profitability in isolation. The only way to keep such a diverse collection of enterprises in place is to keep the whole economy moving forward so a clear signal is sent to everyone. This involves considerable investment to keep a leading edge to replace that which inevitably will become obsolete. Even if large chunks of the economy are evolving from their early-adopter, high-profit stage, to lower-profit commodity stages, the transition has to be handled carefully. A wholesale rush to relocate less profitable business to cheap labour areas to restore profitability, but which reverses the spiral of prosperity, will diminish the prospects for the next generation of enterprises of ever becoming successfully established. Sometimes the only organization that can rise above individual corporate self-interest and see the big picture is the government. If individual companies will not put in the investment then there is no alternative but for the taxpayer to foot the bill. It's their country and they have more commitment to it than multinational corporations. Leaving it to the market to decide can be like standing next to a breach in a dam, watching the water flood out and doing nothing to repair the damage. Successful companies are well-managed companies; successful economies also need managing well.

8

Capitalism Channelled by Technology

The nineteenth century closed leaving a dilemma. Britain had industrialized first and become the workshop of the world, but other nations, especially in Europe, were catching up. First they reclaimed their home markets, and then they too ventured forth on to the world scene in pursuit of their own dreams of wealth, through trade in manufactured goods made possible by the technology of the industrial revolution. The inevitable then happened. Markets everywhere became saturated as the world was presented with more goods than it could pay for. In the industrialized nations low wages were the order of the day and, in Great Britain especially, the entrepreneurs made their money by selling surplus production abroad. The domestic workforces were not paid well enough to absorb their own production.

The years 1873 to 1896 are known as the Great Depression. During this period the industrial economies of Europe stalled and stagnated. New markets had to be found or progress, based on this approach to industrialization, would have run its course. The theories of Thomas Malthus might then have been put to the test with terrible consequences, as the now more numerous working poor found their brief flirtation with industrial technology at an end, and their future once again dependent upon scraping a living on the fringes of society.

The answer to this dilemma did not come from the Old World where old attitudes restricted the way society could be perceived. European leaders automatically accepted that society was a series of hierarchies based on privilege and rank. Most European countries were monarchies, who placed excessive importance on their dignities and their positions at the pinnacle of society. When hierarchies have been in place for too long and they become excessively established, their preservation demands that those under them know and keep their place. As they are no longer going up, so to speak, then the difference must be maintained by keeping the others down. This also translated into a ranking of material entitlements. The poor were poor, and any attempt by them to 'ape their betters' in social behaviour or increased material wealth was greeted with disbelief and derision. In Britain, even in the early twentieth century, the vote was restricted by property rights and denied to women. An unelected hereditary House of Lords could block parliamentary legislation. The 'establishment' was reluctant to give up its comfortable old ways and misplaced sense of superiority, based on having what others had never been able to afford.

The answer came from America where a new world was being built on the basis of equality of opportunity and equal rights. New attitudes, new thoughts, and new ways of doing things were able to be tried out without being suffocated at birth by establishment prejudices and privileges. Henry Ford was one who saw the possibilities.

What Henry Ford and others like him realized was the simple fact that there was no longer any need to search the world for customers. The biggest mass market of all was available right under everyone's noses. Goods made cheaply enough, by workers paid well enough to buy them, offered a self-sustaining market for almost any commodity in almost any quantity. The aristocratic societies of Europe were incapable of such thinking. The very thought of his servant owning a car would have caused an Old World aristocrat to have a seizure.

On 12 August 1908 the first Model T Ford rolled off the production lines. It was deliberately built as a motor car for the masses, selling at $900 or about £200 based on the exchange rates of the time. On 5 January 1914, Henry Ford distributed $10 million out of profits to his workforce and doubled their wages to $5 for an eight-hour day. Thirty-six weeks' pay would buy a worker a car, a ratio not that dissimilar for a modern autoworker. On 21 November 1929, just one month after the Wall Street crash, Henry Ford astonished everyone by announcing a wage increase for the workforce. This was in stark contrast to the advice being given to governments by accountants and economists to cut costs and balance budgets. All they could see of the world was through their books and the rules that they had created for filling them in. What Henry Ford could see was that consumerism cannot exist without consumers, and he knew how to create them.

According to Jeremy Rifkin,[1] the depression in the USA was in part caused by productivity outpacing wages. 'Between 1920 and 1927 productivity in American industry rose by 40 per cent . . . and at the same time 2.5 million jobs disappeared.'

At the height of the depression there were over 15 million American workers unemployed. Many business people recognized that this lack of buying power from so many people was one of the primary causes of the depression. Senator Hugo L. Black of Alabama introduced a 'thirty-hour week bill' as a means of immediately creating an estimated 6.5 million jobs. The bill was passed by the Senate in 1933. America looked as if it might become the first thirty-hour-week economy in the world. President Roosevelt, under pressure from big business, persuaded the legislature to drop the measure in favour of what later became the New Deal, based on job creation through massive government spending on public works.

The prosperity of the industrialized world is now based on this simple arrangement. Jobs make consumers and consumers make jobs. Take away the jobs and you have no consumers. Take away the consumers and you have no jobs. Low wages are the next worst thing to no jobs, because they eventually impoverish the consumers when they have used up all their savings and other reserves. Since the 1930s governments everywhere have been major creators of jobs. Tens of millions of people have depended upon various types of government spending for their jobs or livelihoods. Before the 1930s government spending accounted for around 10 per cent of GDP. Today it accounts for 30 per cent to 40 per cent and more in some countries. This spending and its associated job creation would not take place if left to the workings of a free market. Individuals are under no obligation to spend their wealth.

Not all forms of capitalism recognize this necessary arrangement. Short-term capitalism emphasizes profits in the short term. Profits are maximized fastest by eliminating costs, and one of the biggest costs is in creating consumers by paying good wages. Short-term capitalism expects to find its markets, it does not expect to have to create them. In this respect it is lazy. The maximum short-term profits can be made by manufacturing in the cheapest market and selling in the most expensive market. The maximum long-term sustainable profits arise from maintaining the health of existing high-wage markets by manufacturing in them, and at the same time turning the low-wage markets into high-wage markets as quickly as possible. Competitive advantage, if gained through trade based on low pay, will enrich the trader and impoverish society. If the world's economy is to be based on trade then we must be vigilant to ensure that it is not also based on low pay. The choice is between levelling up or levelling down.

The history of the twentieth century has been one of an increasing

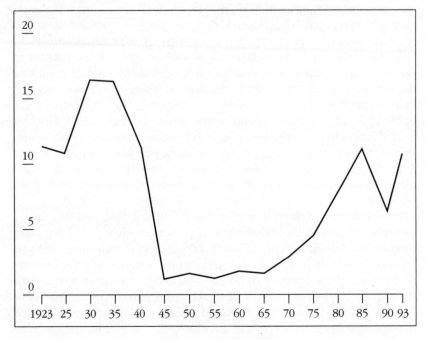

Figure 8.1   *Percentage of UK workforce unemployed*

flow of consumer goods aimed at the mass market of the workers who
also produce them. Some technologies have run their course and died.
Other technologies have reached maturity and no longer offer much by
way of job prospects. However, so far there have always been more than
enough new products and technologies coming through the pipeline to
cancel out these job losses and offer even more relatively well-paid new
jobs as well. Each new production line has come complete with its own
requirement for skilled workers to operate it. Technology until recently
has still compelled the involvement of hundreds of millions of workers
in the wealth-creation process. The spiral created, with help from
government spending to take up the slack, has been virtuous, and whole
populations have benefited from rising standards of living. As a result
of this, and for the first time in modern history, western economies
experienced full employment during the decades of the 1950s, 1960s and
early 1970s. The UK figures in figure 8.1 are typical.

Unfortunately success in one area can simply change the nature of the
problem. Abuse crept into the system in the form of unrealistic wage
demands fuelling inflation. During these decades the public enemy was
now inflation and not unemployment. Some economists, business people

and politicians saw the answer to the new problem of inflation being the maintenance of a reserve army of unemployed, to discipline the expectations of the workforce, and to tip the balance in favour of capital. The polite way of discussing the matter has been to refer to a 'natural level' of unemployment or the 'non-accelerating inflation rate of un-employment' (NAIRU), currently estimated to be around 6 per cent in the USA.[2] It would be electoral suicide to say so in public, but actions speak louder than words. The real danger is that if the politicians over-play their hand in this respect, the whole system will collapse. The misuse and misjudgement of technological change is capable of creating enough unemployment on its own without being helped in this cynical way. The politicians are now running on ideas that lag behind the reality of our fast-moving technological world.

As we approach the twenty-first century our technology is changing, and instead of allowing capitalism based on individual success and the creation of well-paid jobs, it is now in danger of allowing the capitalist to operate best, in the short term at least, by eliminating employment.

US Labour Secretary Robert Reich recognizes this new reality. Reported in the *Vancouver Sun*[3] Reich's position is summarized as follows.

Reich's attack on current orthodox economic thinking was based on re-lease of statistics, the latest in a long stream, showing that while produc-tivity of American business surged by 2.1 per cent in the past year, compensation for workers, mostly salaries, declined by three per cent, the largest drop in eight years.

The trend is not new. Between 1977 and 1992, productivity of American workers increased by 30 per cent while salaries slumped 13 per cent. 'Since the beginning of the recovery, employers have done everything they could to prevent workers from sharing in the prosperity', the labor secretary groused.

'What we are witnessing is that the economy can grow, but average workers can be worse off. The long term question is obvious – if companies are slashing salaries, who's going to be buying their products'?

Car maker Henry Ford once asked the same question and promptly gave his workers a hefty raise. Today's business leaders simply say we'll sell to other people, in other lands.

This same trend is taking place in the UK. Figures released by the Central Statistical Office, 22 September 1995, show that the share of GDP going to wages has dropped to its lowest level since records began in 1955. In the mid 1970s wages accounted for 72 per cent of GDP. In 1995 they accounted for only 62 per cent of GDP. This translates into an income loss of £2,750 a year, or £50 a week, for every worker. At this rate of overall decline, wage increases of 3.25 per cent for those left in work are not enough to keep up with the overall upward drift in prices of 3.6 per cent.[4] Thus the depression feeds upon itself.

The problem, or opportunity, is that a whole new phase of technology is kicking in. In 1981 Hewlett Packard launched the first commercial 32-bit single-chip CPU, with 450,000 transistors on a single piece of silicon measuring 1cm square. In lay terms it was the first computer on a chip. This was a watershed for computer technology and may well be considered as the start of a new era. Until this time, people worked with computer technology doing those things that only people could do, such as making decisions. Even the technology of the computers themselves needed to be operated by large numbers of highly-paid and trained professionals.

The computer on a chip has changed all that. Although not yet intelligent (it is only a matter of time), it no longer requires people to operate it. Computer hardware technology itself has reached the mature stage in its life cycle. This applies to both the users and the producers. A quick look at the employment news from the hardware part of the computer industry for the years 1992 and 1993 says it all. The job losses in the industry during these two years are to be counted in the tens of thousands if not the millions worldwide. It is not just the job losses that make depressing reading, but also the fact that they signal the end of this industry as a major source of new highly-paid mass employment in the future. The pattern of the past has been that as each wave of technology died away, it was replaced by a new one that replaced the jobs and bettered the income lost. A lot of people are banking on this process remaining true, but any optimism that this will happen again will now have to be based on hope as much as anything pragmatic.

The solid-state circuitry of modern computers now hardly ever breaks down, and it can be left alone to run unattended in all manner of environments, on an ever-increasing range of tasks. The price of computing power is falling faster than almost anything else, and the pace of technical change is more rapid than anything experienced previously. When computers were electrical machines with moving parts they occupied whole rooms and were very expensive investments. Their use was limited to high-priority work. Now the power of these machines is all on one or two tiny wafers of silicon that can be mass produced in any one of hundreds of factories world-wide. What used to cost over £1 million can now cost less than £100, and every year costs less still. Jobs that were too expensive to automate yesterday are now next in line to be replaced by these tireless wonders.

People are no longer required to work with technology, they are

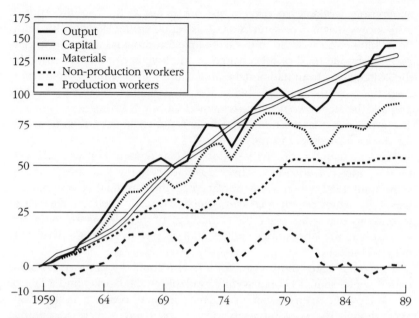

Figure 8.2 *Manufacturing output and input volumes, percentage change since 1959*

Source: Berman, Bound and Griliches, *Quarterly Journal of Economics*, May 1994.

required only to supervise it. In any office or factory there have always been fewer supervisors than workers. We still have jobs for the supervisors but there are not enough jobs for the workers. This is the heart of the dilemma facing us today. If the technology that created mass employment has run its course, what will replace it?

Two hundred years ago the economist Ricardo theorized that when new processes are introduced, the welfare of all would be increased by workers re-training and moving quickly to take advantage of the new opportunities. However, he did not have to contend with the computer. Some experts and politicians still hold to this line of reasoning, and there is a reluctance amongst them to admit that there is any such thing as technological unemployment, even though people working at the grass roots can see it for themselves. However, figure 8.2, and supporting evidence released by the US Bureau of Economic Research, confirms what people working in industry already know.[5]

What the research shows is that, as a result of capital investment in new technology, output has increased faster than raw material inputs because of a more efficient use of·raw materials. It also shows that, as part of the process of upgrading the technology, the demand for skilled supervisory workers has risen, albeit not as fast as the rise in output. It also shows that the new technology is reducing the demand for traditional blue-collar workers at the same time as output is climbing. Furthermore, only one third of this change in employment profile is caused by the switch away from traditional manufacturing to new hi-tech industries. Two thirds of the jobs are being lost in traditional industries as they upgrade their technology in line with modern labour-saving developments. The problem is that the new technology is not creating enough new jobs for displaced workers to move into.

The agricultural economy lasted for 10,000 years until it was replaced by the industrial economy. The industrial economy has lasted for 200 years until 1950, when it was replaced by the information economy. It was 1950 when commercial computers first made their entrance. The technology that will replace the technology of the information economy is already in the laboratories and awaiting its turn to enter our lives. This is biotechnology.

It generally takes thirty years for a new technology to move from the experimental stage to being widely available in the market and a fact of life. Microwave ovens became standard consumer products in the 1980s even though the cooking properties of microwaves were recognized during the Second World War. The principles of television were understood in the 1930s but they did not become a mass market product until the 1960s. Jet engines were invented in the 1940s but did not dominate air travel until the 1970s. It took thirty years for computers to move from being giant machines to the launch of the first desktop Personal Computer in 1980. Biotechnology should be due to take over around the year 2020. The information economy as a creator and destroyer of jobs will have lasted for seventy years. The life cycles of each new phase of our scientific and technical development are becoming shorter. Society hardly has time any more to adjust to the social consequences of the changes.

The introduction now of new technology will create new jobs suited to more skilled or more intelligent people, and we can look forward to this bonus being delivered by new waves of computer technology, and ultimately biotechnology, but it will be for a smaller section of the population than previously. The jobs that are already being lost, particularly amongst the better-paid manual workers and craftsmen and women, stand a very good chance of never being replaced. Our economy is already highly mechanized and it will only become more so. When biotechnology takes over, it could be the turn of the solid-state computers to be replaced, alongside many of the remaining human workers, if that is any consolation.

Each technology creates its own employment patterns. The agricultural economy employs families and its potential is tied back to the availability of land. The industrial economy has employed hundreds of millions of individuals, gathered together at places of work where they function as teams. Indeed the industrial economy encouraged these large populations into existence, because without them the industrial economy would have been resource-constrained by the lack of labour. The work pattern of the information economy is emerging. The information technology-driven economy is having the effect of decentralizing work, as improving communications mean that people no longer need to be in the same place to communicate with each other. Their input can be called upon when it is needed. This is increasing the opportunity for part-time working, as there is no need to keep expensive resources on hand and within earshot, just in case they are required. *Computer Weekly* reports the case of a major international computer company offering its engineers, aged fifty years and above, part-time contracts. A spokesman for the engineers stated 'It is yet another ploy to cut costs without losing essential skills'.[6] Their expertise can be called on only when needed and paid for only as used.

The most extreme example of this behaviour is probably the one discovered by the trades union USDAW. A spokesperson for the union reports instances at the franchise burger chain of Burger King in the UK where staff have been 'encouraged' into clocking on and off the job depending upon the flow of customers. This has resulted in one worker in Glasgow being paid £1 for a five-hour shift.

How real this problem is becoming in the UK is revealed in the Survey of Long Term Employment Strategies undertaken by the Institute of Management.[7] The Institute has over 700 corporate members and over 70,000 individual manager grade members who cover some 3,000,000 workers. The report states:

> The momentum toward a core/complementary pattern of employment is growing, with the majority of large employers embracing the model as integral to future human resource strategies. Six in ten employers predict that at least a quarter of their employees will be complementary to the core work force in four years time. For 17 per cent, half the work-force will be complementary.
>
> Few employers predict a return to traditional patterns of full-time core employment. The trend to contracting out, reported in the previous surveys, continues. Two thirds of large employers expect to contract out more work in the next year . . . Among remaining core staff, work patterns will also continue to change, with increases in part-time work and work sharing.
>
> Employer's decisions on the shape and size of their work-force continue to be motivated by the need to drive down fixed costs.

This already threatens the continuation of the consumer economy. One employer's cost cutting is many employees' reduced spending power. What the employment patterns of a bioeconomy will be are anyone's guess. There could be no paid employment if computers and robots are capable of doing everything. What will sustain the consumer economy then?

9

Demand Deficiency

The world is a place of renewal. Closure of businesses due to competition is harsh, but justifiable in the right circumstances. Competition is designed to force firms to become more efficient. It is a form of progress to see firms close because they will not match the productivity achieved by others. I use the word productivity because it links physical inputs to physical outputs. Financial productivity, in the form of lower costs due to underpaying a workforce or due to distortion by inefficient foreign exchange markets, has a more dubious claim as a measure of efficiency.

However closure due to a 'lack of demand' is something else. In Europe and the USA more food can be produced than can be sold. Farmers are being paid not to grow food and to 'set aside' land and let it return to natural habitat. In this way mountains of food stored at vast expense to the taxpayer are able to be run down and ultimately abolished.

World-wide the pharmaceutical industry is just starting out on a cycle of 'rationalization'. Large international drugs companies are merging or taking over each other. The takeover of The Wellcome Trust by Glaxo is just one example. The justifications are financial. One is that wasteful duplication of research and development can be eliminated and money saved. Another is that product lines can be rationalized and factories closed (up to 25 per cent in one case). Across many different industries the story is the same. Merge the operations, cut out surplus capacity, and make more money supplying the same number of customers from a lower cost base. There is not usually sufficient profitable demand to justify the opposite approach of keeping everything open and supplying many more customers from the same cost base.

However, are there no hungry or starving people in the world? Are there no sick people without medicine? Are there no poor people? Where does the idea come from that productive capacity has to be dismantled because there is no demand for what it can produce? There is plenty of demand. What is lacking for hundreds of millions of people is an effective way of expressing that demand. This is the crucial point. There is a difference between a lack of demand and a deficit in demand. Keynes recognized this point when he advocated counter-cyclical government spending to counteract downturns in the economic cycle.

It may be right to speak of a lack of demand at the micro-economic level. Cash measurements of the cost of inputs and the value of sales are the only effective method yet devised for individual firms to regulate their activities. But the micro-level is not the macro-level. At the macro-level of economics, fundamental questions have to be asked about where demand is coming from. The system is no longer just the sum of its parts. It can be driven by more than just the demand it creates by paying out wages, salaries and even dividends. Given the productivity now available, it needs to be driven by demand other than that it is capable of creating itself. If it is not, then it will simply exist to service the demands of the people it needs to pay, and with evolving technological efficiencies that is a declining number.

Since the depression of the 1930s, advanced societies have recognized that they have a responsibility to correct deficits in demand suffered by the more vulnerable groups in their populations. Only the well-paid can afford to pay for education, health and also to provide for old age. There is simply not the free money available for these things if you are low-paid. So far these deficits in demand have been financed by transfer payments, or taxes, from the relatively rich to the relatively poor. As long as those in work have been the majority of the population and have been well paid then this system has been able to work. However, modern technology is changing the balance and threatening the very foundations of this system. Consider tables 9.1 and 9.2.

Clearly those households earning less than £175 do not have enough to live on and require various measures of income support. Those households earning towards the middle and top of the £175–£375 group will be self-supporting, except for large items such as health care and education which, in the UK, are provided as national services. Those households earning above £375 could have money to spare. Overall, it looks like the top third supporting the bottom third with the middle holding its own. This is the crux of the matter. If the middle section declines into poverty then the top third will be left to support the remaining two thirds, which may prove politically impossible.

Table 9.1   *Low and high incomes*

Percentage of households by weekly income 1992

Under £80	£80–£175	£175–£375	£375–£649	£649+
12.3%	21.8%	30.5%	24.2%	11.4%

Table 9.2   *Distribution of household disposable income*

Quintile groups 1990–1991

Bottom fifth	Next fifth	Middle fifth	Next fifth	Top fifth
7%	12%	17%	23%	41%

At the time of writing, the average weekly wage in manufacturing employment in the UK for men is £288. This is right in the centre of the middle range of earnings. Out of all the changes in employment patterns over the years one stands out above all the others. Since 1970 manufacturing employment has halved by four million and service industry employment has doubled by four million. Service industry employment as far as these displaced employees are concerned tends to pay a lot less than their previous jobs. Advertisements for retail counter jobs and cleaning jobs that make up a growing number of the new service jobs pay wages well under the £175 per week level. The centre is in danger of crumbling and the pieces are already falling downwards, placing an intolerable burden on the remaining taxpayers. There may still be an impressive number of people in work but they are becoming polarized between well paid and badly paid. The badly paid are not able to contribute and may well be recipients of state support. The well paid are a comparatively small group who resent carrying the whole burden.

In the case of low-paid workers, their rates of pay are often just too low to sustain family life or at times life itself. This makes it necessary for the government to top up low wages to minimum levels where people can afford the essential basics of life. In Britain this system is called Family Credits. In line with rising numbers of people working for low pay, the amount of government funds allocated to Family Credits doubled between 1991 and 1993 to £1 billion, and it is set to increase by another 50 per cent in 1994. The number of families who have their incomes from low-paying jobs or unscrupulous employers topped up in this way has risen from 326,000 to 521,000.

It might be legitimate, in this instance, to ask if the policy makers have studied history and if they have ever heard the name of Speenhamland. In the last century there were workers who were receiving wages that were insufficient to buy enough bread to sustain life. The magistrates in the parish of Speenhamland, in what is modern-day Berkshire, levied a parish rate to top up local wages to the subsistence level. Low pay was endemic throughout the economy and so this practice spread rapidly until half the parishes in England were subsidizing the wages of the poor. Unfortunately this put the bad employers paying poor wages at a competitive advantage, and forced the good employers to reduce the wages they paid and so increase the burden on the parish ratepayers. The system lasted for thirty years, until it collapsed under the weight of abuse that is built into systems of this sort. It was followed by the hated 'poor laws', which took the alternative approach of blaming the poor for their own condition, and subjecting them to what we now would consider extreme criminal abuse in the name of encouraging them to find work. Needless to say, this did not work either, although it satisfied the political prejudices of the right-wingers of the day.

People who work part-time or are low-paid don't pay tax. The Low Pay Network calculated in a specific instance that 91 part-time jobs being offered by a local retailer at an average wage of £39.05p for 11.36 hours work a week, would contribute in taxation to the UK Government in total just £1,470 per annum. If these jobs had been 28 equivalent full-time positions the tax yield would have been £41,918 per year.

Consequently the burden falls on those people who can afford to pay tax, and this prompts an equally important consideration. At what point does tax on income cease to be acceptable and instead become a deterrent to work and enterprise?

Table 9.3 shows, for a variety of countries, both the tax taken from individuals and the total tax taken from the whole economy. These figures show the tax burdens on various populations and indicate a preference for direct or indirect taxation in the different countries. Total government spending can be higher because borrowings are not taken into account. The USA may have been getting away with the lowest taxes only because it has been running the world's largest budget deficits. In 1980 the US public debt stood at $907 billion, in 1993 it stood at $4,351 billion or nearly nine months GDP equivalent.

The problem is that for many countries, particularly those with the most generous social policies, the correction of demand deficit for the needy groups in their populations by tax transfers has probably reached

---

Table 9.3 *Relative taxation by country*

Country	Tax on earnings	All taxes as a percentage of GDP
Denmark	38.5%	50%
Sweden	29%	49%
Luxembourg	19.4%	48%
Netherlands	31.5%	48%
Finland	32%	46%
Norway	31.4%	45%
Belgium	36.1%	45%
France	24.6%	44%
Austria	26.4%	42%
Italy	31.1%	42%
Germany	34%	40%
United Kingdom	31.3%	34%
Switzerland	20.6%	32%
USA	21%	29%

Source: OECD and UBS

its limits. In the UK the need to widen the tax net and so spread the burden has reached ridiculous proportions. Incomes that are below the official poverty level are taxed on the one hand and, on the other hand, those same people receive state benefits to give them back enough money to live on. Even the relatively well-off have something to complain about. The highest rate of tax kicks in at 40 per cent on taxable incomes of just £24,300, which is only just above the average for all incomes.

Unemployment pay does take its share of the tax cake, but overall it is only a minority of the redistribution. The vast majority is made up of pensions for people no longer in the workforce, the education of the young, the care of the sick and so on. It is not possible to solve this problem by blaming and penalizing the unemployed or any other sector of the population. It is only possible to relieve the tax burden on the well-off by cutting back on the basic social provisions made for vulnerable groups. If we do that, then we will further exaggerate the deficit in demand that is developing and further collapse those sections of the economy that depend on that demand.

There is a perfectly fair argument to be made for leaving more of the money that the people earn in the people's pockets. However that is a different issue from the one we are discussing here. The top 40 per cent of households already have 64 per cent of the disposable income. That discretionary spending is not doing anything to halt the growth in poverty that is clearly taking place amongst the weaker groups in society. Why should further tax cuts at the top add anything more to the solution? If the well-off spend on imports, or buy goods manufactured in robotic factories, or hoard their wealth, there will be no trickle-down to other groups in society.

The biggest mistake that we can make in present circumstances is to think that running an economy is just like running a company or indeed just like running a family budget. At the micro-level, we can think in terms of balancing money in and money out. If we chop the economy up into sectors we can still think in this way. However, at the macro-level we have to learn to think differently. A highly automated economy run on purely competitive lines does not need to employ and pay people in step with what it produces. Because of this, the more automated an economy becomes, the more it will suffer from a deficit in demand from those people it no longer needs to employ. This is the new dilemma.

10

Do Other Cultures Behave Differently?

The British and American cultural heritage places great value on the individual, and the maximum freedom of the individual, to pursue his or her self-interest, even at the expense of community or other shared values. The individual ranks before society. In Margaret Thatcher's often quoted remark 'There is no such thing as society, only families'.

Against this background companies are the vehicles through which individuals express their economic self-interests. The principal stakeholders in British and American companies are the shareholders. They appoint Boards of Directors and Chief Executive Officers to maximize the profits on their investments. Employees are hired and fired in the service of this objective, and each employee is responsible for negotiating his own deal. Market forces determine the relative strengths and weaknesses of the parties in this adversarial bargaining process.

The role of the stock market in Britain and America emphasizes the need for companies to concentrate on delivering short-term profitability. Table 10.1[1] shows the dominant role of listed companies in both countries compared to Japan and Germany. In this 'market-driven' system the value of shares is a multiple of the quarterly or annual profits. Companies driven in this way have to be very careful about damaging their short-term profits by spending heavily on long-term investments and such things as Research and Development. They must watch very carefully their cost base, especially their labour costs. They cannot afford the luxury of creating additional customers by adopting generous employment policies. They have to assume that demand exists independently from their employment practices, if necessary created by the government

Table 10.1 *Role of listed companies*

	GDP ($ billion)	Stock market capitalization	Percentage relationship
UK	1,025	832	81.7
USA	5,905	4,757	80.5
Japan[a]	3,508	2,399	68.3
Germany	1,846	348	18.8

[a] Japanese shares trade on a higher Price/Earnings ratio than the other markets which over emphasizes their capitalization in this example.

or some other agency. It is a versatile and reactive system in the hunt for profits. The metaphor of the hunter is appropriate when it is compared to other cultural approaches.

Britain, America, Canada and Australia share a similar form of capitalism.[2] However, each nation that has a cultural identity twists or tweaks capitalism to fit its own particular values. Since the demise of communism as the enemy, the differing interpretations of the capitalist model are competing for supremacy. The 'Anglo-Saxon' model may have a head start due to the historical importance of Britain and America in world trade, but it is still in the minority and the race is still being run. It is not the purpose of this book to explore all the variations of capitalism on offer. Instead I have selected two further models to illustrate what is possible and to give a clue as to which may be the eventual winners.

The German model of capitalism differs from the Anglo-Saxon model and is based on 'community logic', also referred to as the 'social market economy'. The stockmarket, with its short-term profit imperatives, is much less important and so there is room for interests other than profits to play a major part. Companies are able to serve the community as well as serve the interests of their owners. A richer community can in turn make it easier for companies to prosper. The recognition that there are more stakeholders than just the shareholders is reflected in the way that German company law organizes its companies.[3]

The larger companies are organized around a two-tier board structure. The *Aufsichtsrat* is the supervisory board. In these larger companies the representation on this board is drawn equally from shareholder representatives, and representatives of the employees, either directly or indirectly via union representation. Amongst the shareholder representatives will often be found a representative of the 'house bank'. German banks own shares in many of their client companies. The *Aufsichtsrat* appoints the *Vorstand* to run the company and is then forbidden by law from interfering directly in the running of the company.

The *Vorstand* is the managerial board. Its members are appointed for fixed periods and are drawn from the management team of the company. They run the company and are legally responsible for the good stewardship of the enterprise. Their style is largely collegiate and they liaise very closely with works councils so that the entire workforce is apprised of the affairs of the company.

Unless a company is getting into trouble the balance of power rests with the *Vorstand*. This gives rise to the following business ethos and priorities which are shared with the *Aufsichtsrat*.

1   The legal obligation for the good stewardship of the company and its long-term survival are of prime importance. Pensions are often not separately funded and pension money can form part of the working capital of the enterprise, making the long-term viability and survival of the enterprise in everyone's best interests. Long-term survival places a high priority on capital investment and on training the workforce in the latest techniques.

2   Customers guarantee the survival of a company and good customers are attracted and retained by quality. German products have a world-wide reputation for good quality.

3   Employees ultimately make or break a company. Sensible behaviour in relation to wage bargaining helps keep the company viable, but at the same time the employees expect to share in the success of the company, and German workers are now amongst the best-paid in the world.

4   Shareholders deserve their reward too, but only after the health of the company has been secured.

5   Hostile takeovers and the casual buying and selling of companies is unacceptable. It is akin to buying and selling people and playing fast and loose with important parts of the fabric of the community.

In Britain there have been periodic campaigns extolling people to 'Buy British'. In Germany the slogan is 'Make it in Germany', and it is taken seriously. The more work that there is in the community, the more the community prospers, and so the firms that serve the community also prosper more. In relation to the Anglo-Saxon hunter, German industry is a farmer who harvests profits, but not without planting next year's crop. This system may be less able to react quickly to change, a little less exciting, a little more fenced in by rules and regulations, but it is more stable and it delivers steady growth.

If the British and American model of capitalism is at the individualistic end of the spectrum, and the German model is in the communitarian middle of the spectrum, then the Japanese model is at the community/ group end of the spectrum. Westerners can have some difficulty in understanding the Japanese mindset and their way of looking at individuals in relation to society. It is just different. Almost in direct opposition to Margaret Thatcher's remark, a Japanese leader might comment 'There is no such thing as an individual, only groups'. The individual has no identity worth talking about except as a member of a group. Within groups and between groups what matters are the relationships. The members of a group support each other and groups which share relationships also support each other. Companies are composed of work groups that have relationships with each other, and companies themselves have relationships with other companies within a larger grouping. The ultimate group is that of being Japanese. It is entirely natural in the Japanese mind to think first of the welfare of the group, secondly to promote the welfare of the group and thirdly to promote, or defend, the welfare of other groups with whom relationships exist. It is alien to think of one's self as an individual and to seek individual profit at the expense of the group.

Japanese groups are outward-looking[4] and seek to establish suitable relationships with as many other groups as possible. One of the most important groups is that of the customers. Success is not judged by the amount of profit that can be wrested from the customer, but instead it is judged by the strength of the relationship formed with the customer and by the number of successful relationships formed. The Japanese also have a strong sense of obligation. If you do something for me then I am obligated to do something for you, and so the relationship is strengthened. The more you do for me, even unasked, then the more I am obligated to you in return. Commercially this translates into finding new ways of giving the customer more and more value, in return for which the customer rewards the supplier with his loyalty. Profits then flow from strong relationships and the more people you serve, the more strong relationships you have.

To accuse the Japanese of acting uncompetitively in relation to the Western concept of 'free market' economics as proposed by Adam Smith is to miss the point. If one company within a group is facing strong competitive pressures then other companies within that same group will help it to fight off the competition by such tactics as lowering the prices of components or other services that they supply to their beleaguered member. The market is a secondary mechanism coming behind the formation (and maintaining or defending) of good relationships.

This way of thinking is also reflected in other business areas. The British and American way of doing business is to 'go for the contract'. The contract marks the start of the business relationship, it defines the scope of the relationship and its purpose is the generation of profits. Disputes over contract terms and performance are a major feature of the American business scene. The German collegiate style places more emphasis on fitting in, understanding the requirements, sharing the same values and accepting the same rules. This can take time. Only after you have been accepted is a contract signed and, with typical German thoroughness, you are then expected to deliver to the precise terms of the contract. In contrast to both these approaches, the Japanese spend enormous lengths of time building up the relationship. Meetings that seem to get nowhere and polite remarks that have hidden meanings, can frustrate the 'go-getting' British and American salesman to the point of despair. However, what the Japanese are doing in these long drawn out preliminaries is deciding if you are the sort of person that they can trust, and who will invest as much into the relationship as they will, over a considerable period of time. If you are, then they will eventually sign a contract. However, they know that there is more to a successful relationship than can ever be expressed in a legal document. Indeed, if the relationship changes then they would expect the contract to change as well. The contract is a memorandum of the relationship at a point in time, not the all-defining start and end of things. When British Aerospace plc sold its Rover car subsidiary to BMW without telling its minority partner, Honda, the hurt felt by Honda was not just the commercial betrayal but the fact that they had invested so much in a relationship that was summarily cast aside.

However, the question to be answered now is which approach is likely to be the more successful? Rather than look at all the possible economic indicators, I have chosen in tables 10.2–10.4 to look at a selection of figures that also reflect aspects of the 'quality of life'.

There is little doubt that the economic superstars of the last three decades have been Germany and Japan. From ruined economies after World War Two they have caught up with and are in the process of overtaking America. Could it be that protection from the more destructive kinds of market forces, particularly the demands of the stock market, have helped rather than hindered growth? Although Japan's stock market capitalization appears very high, stability is introduced by related companies taking cross-shareholdings in each other, which restricts the number of shares in general circulation and defeats the unwelcome attentions of hostile bidders.

It is also interesting to note the way GDP is generated in the four

Table 10.2   *Per capita GDP*

Country	$
Japan	28,217
USA	23,113
Germany	22,917
UK	17,760

Source: *Pocket World in Figures*, 1995

Table 10.3   *Generation of GDP*

Country	Manufacturing	All Industry	Services
Japan	29%	42%	55%
Germany	33%	37%	58%
UK	20%	31%	67%
USA	18%	24%	73%

Source: *Pocket World in Figures*, 1995

Table 10.4   *Wage differential between the CEOs and the lowest-paid workers in their companies*

Country	Differential
USA	85 times
UK	33 times
Germany	25 times
Japan	17 times

Source: Michel Albert, *Capitalism Against Capitalism*, 1993

economies, and the split between industry, manufacturing and services. Japan and Germany traditionally run large balance of payments surpluses, whilst the UK and USA traditionally run equally large deficits, suggesting that an emphasis on industry and manufacturing is still the key to financial independence. Services are not as easy to trade as physical goods.

However, what matters to individuals is how much they benefit personally in return for their labours. Wealth, and hierarchies built around wealth, exist in all societies, but most people depend upon their individual earning power for their economic well-being. Table 10.4 is a guide to how the money earned by companies is shared amongst those who helped generate the wealth.[5]

Taking all these figures into consideration, Japan would appear to be the winner, but appearances can be deceptive. The cost of living is very high in Japan and living space is in short supply. More importantly, the Japanese sense of obligation has one consequence that is distinctly unappealing to many Westerners. If the company looks after its workers well, they in turn are obligated to repay the company by putting in extra work, even if that extra work simply means sitting at a desk doing nothing useful long into the evening. A first-hand and revealing account of living and working in Japan, as seen through Western eyes, is given in Katzenstein's *Funny Business.*[6] For many people, the author included, there has to be a sensible balance between working to live and living to work.

Another side to Japanese groups are the consequences of being excluded. The world-renowned Japanese companies that offer their workers security employ about one third of the workforce. Most of the rest of the workers are employed by the subcontractors that supply the large groups. When times get tough the large groups pass their problems back down the supply chain to the subcontractors. It is the subcontractors who have to lay off labour as the major companies pull work back in house to keep their own staff busy. It is the subcontractors who have to deliver smaller quantities at lower prices to help the major companies become more competitive. Even in the seemingly more egalitarian Japanese economy there is a pecking order.

However, long hours are not the exclusive preserve of the Japanese worker. The British and American economies suffer from the same problem. In America in all but one of the twenty-five categories of manufacturing industry, listed hours worked per week have risen, not fallen, since 1975. In the most extreme cases the increase has been in the order of 10 per cent, from approximately forty hours to forty-four hours.[7] The UK is home to half of all the workers in the European Community who work more than forty-eight hours per week.[8] In both countries this is against a background of high and persistent unemployment. German workers, in contrast, enjoy the shortest working week of any European country with an average of thirty-seven hours. The German economy is going through difficulties and there is unemployment. However, when Volkswagen was faced with a dramatic fall in demand it chose to introduce a four-day week and preserve 30,000 jobs rather than add to the unemployment figures and misery.

Of the different cultural approaches it appears that Germany offers the best combination of high wages and the leisure time to enjoy what has been earned. In contrast, the British and American economies offer the able individual the greatest opportunity to succeed spectacularly, whilst rewarding the less able or the unlucky with a diminishing share of what is available. In contrast to both, the top Japanese companies are more egalitarian in their rewards, they look after their workers 'from cradle to grave' and they create new jobs for their employees when technology moves on. Indeed it is the persistently high Japanese investment in new technology that is ensuring that their companies and workers are tomorrow's winners.

In the rapidly growing area of the Pacific Rim it appears that, like Japan, the most vigorously growing economies are the ones that combine a strong, if at times flawed, sense of community with a strong business ethic. The Tiger economies of the Far East fall into this category. Countries that have one but not both of these features do less well. Countries such as the USA and the UK that have a strong individualistic business ethic, but lack a sense of shared community objectives, are not matching the growth rates of the Pacific Tigers. Countries that have a strong sense of family or community, such as Spain or Greece, but lack such a strong business ethic perform less well too.[9]

However, technology is having one other important effect. It is shrinking the world. Cultures that were protected by long sea voyages and infrequent foreign visitors are now exposed to cultural and business contacts that mix millions of people together on a daily basis. No society is an island any more and, although some strive to hold on to their cultural uniqueness more than others, there is a relentless move towards convergence. In particular, those economies such as Japan and Germany, that have been able to avoid the worst horrors of high and persistent unemployment are under great pressure from competitors, who place less value on employment rights and the social conditions of their workforces.

11

Multinational Companies, Global Companies and International Trade

In addition to technology radically reshaping the world of work, we also have to contend with the activities of both multinational companies and global companies. Here, technology in the forms of instantaneous communications and fast, efficient transport links is shrinking the world to the extent that some writers feel able to talk of the 'global village'. This may be a little exaggerated in the case of the provision of physical goods, but it is increasingly true for the knowledge-based industries, where software can be downloaded over international data links and banks can transfer billions of dollars instantaneously across national frontiers.

The growth in importance of multinational and global companies can be tracked by the evolution of one type of computer software. In the late 1970s and early 1980s the pressure was on to deliver and install 'material requirements planning', or MRP software, because firms were wasting huge amounts of money ordering the wrong amounts of materials, for delivery at the wrong time. In the mid 1980s, with this problem solved, the emphasis changed to 'manufacturing requirements planning', or MRP II, which relates the physical capacity of a company to produce products back into the ordering process. Both these computerized techniques relate, in the main, to single factory sites. Now in the 1990s, the race is on between software companies to deliver 'distribution requirements planning', or DRP software. This software handles the allocation of production across multiple sites which can be situated anywhere in the world, from customer orders that can come from anywhere in the world. Multinational companies are now planning for a future where they can sell in every country, whilst producing in just a few.

The problem is that the increasing globalization of the world's economy is redefining the relationship between economic activity that is internal to a national economy and that which is external, namely international trade. It is the level and quality of economic activity within an economy that principally determines the economic well-being of a population. International trade can be constructive or destructive to that well-being. When trade is for items that the home economy cannot produce for itself, then it is constructive. Trade can even bring a welcome dose of competition to sluggish domestic industries. However, when trade becomes the driving force, with profit its only objective, then it can be wholly destructive to a domestic economy, as production is arbitrarily switched around the world in search of competitive advantage.

There is a difference between multinational and global companies even if, in practice, most large companies are a mixture of both. Multinational companies operate within national economies. They both make and sell in the same economy. They put employment into the economy as well as taking revenue out of the economy. Their influence can be good. They can bring new competition, new products and new ideas to situations that need revitalizing. Over a period of years they can merge into the fabric of the domestic economy such that people no longer see them as foreign firms.

Global companies are different. They have more of the trader about them. They seek to profit by exploiting the difference in costs that exists between economies. Increasingly this means between economic regions and between the rich, developed world and the poor, undeveloped world. It is a trade that benefits neither world in the longer term. A modern factory paying low wages in the Third World does not create consumers there, and its output, exported to First World countries, pushes an equivalent number of employees out of better-paid jobs, thereby gradually impoverishing the rich economy. The difference goes into increasing the profits of the trader.

It can be seen in table 11.1 that General Motors is the largest company in the world with a sales revenue of $132.8 billion. The Iranian economy is 24th in the world in terms of GDP, at $131 billion. The Japanese electronics firm, NEC, is the 40th largest company in the world with sales of $28.4 billion. This is marginally more than Morocco which ranks at number 55 with a GDP of $27 billion. In other words, international companies are now larger than all but the largest of the world's economies.[1]

These companies, if they are global traders, have all the power and little of the responsibility that national governments have towards their populations. In particular they have no long-term responsibility to create customers in either the markets where they sell their goods, or the markets where they manufacture their goods, and so close the loop referred to in chapter 8. As national borders diminish in importance within regional groupings such as the European Economic Community or the North American Free Trade Area, companies could become more important than governments.

Not all international companies are global in their approach to profits. All companies are motivated by profit but, as in social market economies, sometimes companies can also be motivated by other concerns. However, with most global companies there is no room for anything else. Global companies may still be run by people, and people can have allegiances to the societies in which they were born and educated. This can act as a restraint upon the more excessive behaviour that these global giants might indulge in. However, increasingly this link too is being broken for the decision makers who matter. High-flying executives in global companies no longer spend their working lives in one corporate division in one country. They are moved around the world to gain experience of working in different environments. It is entirely natural today to find a British company with an American or French chief executive, and the position is reciprocated. (There are no obvious examples of a major Japanese company employing a non-Japanese person in a similar position.) Thus the ties back to a society and its citizens are weakened, and the gap created is filled by professional ethics. The professional ethics of global management puts profits first and last with nothing else in between. Companies and managers are judged by the profits that they can deliver. Nothing else matters.

Both multinational and global companies seek to maximize their profits. The difference between them is that the former puts more back into the economy in which it operates than does the latter. They both try to take advantage of their international status to minimize their tax liabilities. If too much profit is being generated in a high-tax country, it can be spirited away to a tax haven with a few clever entries in a ledger. Most multinationals trade products between companies within the group as well as with the outside world. This is called inter-company trading. The goods supplied to a profitable factory by another company within the same group can be invoiced through a shell company in a tax haven, and have their value artificially increased. At a stroke a profitable factory can be reduced to break-even levels of profitability on which no tax is due. Head office management charges can also be invented and invoiced.

There are many ways international accounts can be manipulated and there are many highly paid accountants constantly thinking up new ways to do it. However, the wider issue is that if companies are not putting money back into an economy by paying wages and salaries because of

Table 11.1 Economic strength

Biggest economies (GDP, $bn)

Rank	Country	GDP	Rank	Country	GDP
1	United States	5,905		UAE	37
2	Japan	3,508	50	Egypt	35
3	Germany	1,846	51	Nigeria	33
4	France	1,279	52	Hungary	31
5	Italy	1,187	53	Belorussia	30
6	United Kingdom	1,025	54	Kazakhstan	29
7	Canada	566	55	Morocco	27
8	Spain	548	56	Bangladesh	25
9	China	442		Czech Republic	25
10	Brazil	424		Libya	25
11	Russia	398		Romania	25
12	Netherlands	312	60	Puerto Rico	24
13	Australia	299	61	North Korea	23
14	South Korea	296	62	Iraq[a]	22
15	Mexico	295		Kuwait	22
16	India	272	64	Peru	21
17	Switzerland	249	65	Uzbekistan	18
18	Sweden	233	66	Syria	15
19	Belgium	210		Tunisia	15
20	Taiwan	207	68	Luxembourg	14
21	Argentina	200	69	Bulgaria	12
22	Austria	175		Ecuador	12
23	Denmark	134		Slovenia	12
24	Iran	131	72	Oman	11

Largest businesses (by sales, $bn)

Rank	Business	Country	Sales
1	General Motors	United States	132.8
2	Exxon	United States	103.5
3	Ford Motor	United States	100.8
4	Royal Dutch/Shell Group	United Kingdom/Netherlands	98.9
5	Toyota Motor[a]	Japan	79.1
6	IRI[a]	Italy	67.5
7	IBM	United States	65.1
8	Daimler-Benz	Germany	63.3
9	General Electric	United States	62.2
10	Hitachi[a]	Japan	61.5
11	British Petroleum	United Kingdom	59.2
12	Matsushita Electrical Industrial[a]	Japan	57.5
13	Mobil	United States	57.4
14	Volkswagen	Germany	56.7
15	Siemens[a]	Germany	51.4
16	Nissan Motor[a]	Japan	50.2
	Philip Morris	United States	50.2
18	Samsung	South Korea	49.6
19	Fiat	Italy	47.9
20	Unilever	United Kingdom/Netherlands	44.0
21	ENI	Italy	40.4
22	Elf Aquitaine[a]	France	39.7

25	Saudi Arabia	126
26	Indonesia	123
27	Finland	116
28	Turkey	114
29	Norway	110
30	Thailand	107
31	South Africa	106
32	Hong Kong	89
33	Ukraine	87
34	Greece	75
	Poland	75
36	Portugal	73
37	Israel	68
38	Venezuela	59
39	Malaysia	52
40	Pakistan	49
	Philippines	49
42	Algeria	48
43	Colombia	45
44	Myanmar	44
	Singapore	44
46	Ireland	43
47	New Zealand	41
48	Chile	37

73	Cameroon	10
	Guatemala	10
	Slovakia	10
	Uruguay	10
77	Côte d'Ivoire	9
	Qatar	9
	Sri Lanka	9
	Vietnam	9
	Zaire	9
82	Angola[a]	8
	Croatia[a]	8
	Dominican Republic	8
	Kenya	8
86	Cyprus	7
	Ghana	7
	Yemen	7
89	Azerbaijan	6
	Costa Rica	6
	El Salvador	6
	Ethiopia	6
	Iceland	6
	Panama	6
	Paraguay	6
	Senegal	6

23	Nestlé	Switzerland	39.1
24	Chevron	United States	38.5
25	Toshiba[a]	Japan	37.5
26	E.I. Du Pont de Nemours	United States	37.4
27	Texaco	United States	37.1
28	Chrysler	United States	36.9
29	Renault[a]	France	33.9
30	Honda Motor[a]	Japan	33.4
31	Philips Electronics	Netherlands	33.3
32	Sony[a]	Japan	31.5
33	Asea Brown Boveri	Sweden/Switzerland	30.5
	Alcatel Alsthom	France	30.5
35	Boeing	United States	30.4
36	Procter & Gamble[a]	United States	29.9
37	Hoechst	Germany	29.6
38	Peugeot	France	29.4
39	BASF	Germany	28.5
40	NEC[a]	Japan	28.4

[a] Estimate.

the labour-free technology they can now use, then they can still put it back in, albeit reluctantly, via taxation, unless they are amongst the growing band of multinational corporations without any national allegiances, which can put their profits beyond the reach of governments.

In 1994 *The Sunday Times*[2] revealed that the Inland Revenue were targeting multinational companies for over £1 billion of tax from operating revenues that they believe had been wrongfully 'moved' offshore to avoid the UK taxes. More recently *The Independent*,[3] in an exclusive article on its rival, the News International organization, revealed that in the ten years from 1985 to 1995 the company had paid virtually no tax despite having made nearly £1 billion in profit. It was all done by accountants creating a paper chase of loans and debts in associated companies in different tax jurisdictions so that profits in one area could be offset against specially manufactured liabilities in another area. All of this is apparently perfectly legal and is available to any international organization. When asked why every company did not avail itself of these tax-efficient tricks one accountant remarked that some companies are better advised than others.

The extent to which multinational corporations now control the world's productive assets is substantial, and it is growing greater as technology creates a world wherein it is almost quicker to fly between London and New York than it is to commute in and out of either city from their outer suburbs. The world's top 600 corporations today are responsible for 20 per cent of all the world's output and own 20 per cent of the world's productive assets. Just 600 chief executives and their boards of directors can control the destinies of one in every five workers in the world's corporate economic system. Most of these corporations are publicly quoted on Stock Exchanges, but some are privately held and their accounts are never published. All of them are rootless to a greater or lesser extent because they operate globally and find difficulty in owing allegiance to any one national economic entity. Their shareholders can be drawn from the four corners of the earth. With no allegiance to any higher authority, profits have become the sole objective of their operations.

How far can the search for profitability through low wages be pushed? Take the case of China and her emerging economic power. In a recent paper, Professor Lardy of the University of Washington[4] has pointed out that between 1980 and 1991 the Chinese economy grew at an annual rate of 9.4 per cent. It is now the 11th largest exporter in the world. In 1991 it received $5 billion of foreign investment. In 1993 it received $26 billion of foreign investment which went into firms that accounted for 25 per cent of China's exports and 70 per cent of her export growth.

Today 80 per cent of China's population works on the land. By the year 2010, 50 per cent of the population will live in the cities and only 50 per cent will be left in the self-supporting rural environment.[5] In a re-run of the British experience 200 years ago of agricultural labour moving to employment in the factory system, but on a much larger scale, by the year 2000 there will be 268 million unemployed people in China. That is a lot of people who will be willing to work at anything for very low wages.

However, China is not the only emerging economic power in this respect. Professor Stephane Garelli of the World Competitiveness Project[6] alerts us to the fact that the industrialized nations employ some 350 million workers at an average hourly wage of $18, but that in the less developed world there is already a labour force of 1,200 million paid an average hourly wage of less than $2. There is no shortage of companies in both goods and services willing to dump their high-cost labour and exploit this enormous and growing pool of low-paid workers.

Is this just an academic talking point? No – it is frighteningly real. I quote from two interviews given by prominent industrialists to the *Financial Times*.

> Morgan Crucible, the UK speciality materials group, yesterday became the latest international manufacturer to cite labour costs as the reason for shifting production from Western Europe to low wage economies in Asia and Eastern Europe.
>
> The company, which is one of the world's largest suppliers of industrial carbons and ceramics, said it planned to move output from the Netherlands, France and Belgium to plants in Hungary, the Czech Republic, China and Vietnam.
>
> Some 3,000 workers . . . are expected to be affected over 10 years.
>
> Morgan Crucible, which yesterday reported a 20 per cent increase in first half profits . . . predicted that other manufacturers would be forced to reduce operations in high cost countries to improve profit margins.
>
> Justifying Morgan Crucible's decision Mr Bruce Farmer, managing director, said average labour costs in Eastern Europe were $1.50 per hour, compared with $26 an hour in Germany. Moreover, it was paying workers at its new Shanghai plant $1 a day, compared with $31 an hour in Japan. Mr Farmer predicted cost savings would release funds to invest in new plant and machinery, while helping to drive profit margins beyond 14 per cent by 1997.
>
> The need to cut labour costs was also highlighted by British Polythene Industries (BPI), Europe's largest polythene film producer. BPI, which yesterday reported interim pre tax profits up from £8.61m to £11.5m, said it had to move production from Britain to China to keep its share of the world carrier bag market. Workers at the group's factory in China's Guangdong province are being paid a total of $1,000 a year. Workers at its

Telford plant in the (British) Midlands, by comparison, were taking home up to £15,000 a year before the decision was taken to close it in February. Mr McLatchie commented 'It's very regrettable, but all manufacturers are being driven this way by market conditions.'[7]

I challenge any politician or economist to explain to Western workers how they can be competitive in these circumstances, or how they can live off $1 a day. To believe that the free workings of the free market will automatically deliver the best solution is nothing short of blind prejudice when faced with this reality.

Historically some protection was offered by the cost of transport, and the lack of capacity to transport large amounts of products around the world. The large container ships of today are a modern invention. If you go to the docks in Bristol you will find there the first iron steamship, *S.S. Great Britain*, built by Brunel in 1843. Just look at the amount of space that could be devoted to cargo – it is surprisingly small. One or two modern articulated trucks could carry more. Today journey times are seldom more than six weeks between the major economies of East and West, and cargo capacities can be measured in tens of thousands of tonnes.

Commodity products such as hand tools, garden spades, rubber gloves or any item that is sold to the public 'as is', with no further variations, are prime candidates for being manufactured with cheap labour and shipped to richer markets. Products that have to be finished, or adapted, are not so easy. Today consumers change their minds rapidly and will only buy what they want, when they want it. Clothes are an example. They are driven by fashion trends which can come and go over a period of weeks. Consequently, the low-value base textile can be manufactured in the Third World, but the finishing, such as dyeing, making up, etc., has to be done close to the consumer. This preserves some jobs in the richer economies, but in this example they too tend to be in the lower-paid sector.

Alarmingly, this phenomenon is being reversed in the hi-tech industries. It might have been supposed that the finishing of products, especially in hi-tech goods, being relatively skilled, might keep some well-paid jobs in the richer economies. Not so! Fate is playing a perverse trick here. Computers have to be configured to customer specification by adding extra circuit boards or other refinements before they can be sold. Customers are rarely willing to wait more than a few days for what they want. The outer casings are the low-tech, heavy, bulky commodity items that might be expected to be shipped in from low-wage manufacturers. Again, not so. The customer will not wait six weeks, and manufacturers, working to JIT schedules, will not carry this amount of stock.

Consequently, these low-value items are made locally. The really clever, high-value circuit boards are light and compact. They can be air-freighted in a matter of hours from any part of the globe. Thus there is no room for the skilful and well-educated sectors of the population of the rich world to become complacent. Graduates from universities on the Indian subcontinent are just as clever as graduates from Oxford or Harvard, and they work for a fraction of the wage that their western counterparts expect. British Airways has located a significant part of its computerized ticketing system in India. It is just one of a growing number of companies relocating their data-processing operations to the subcontinent. In Britain it has been traditional for millions of people to save their money in building societies. Until recently their savings were recorded in books that were filled in at the local branch. These same people would be surprised to know that some societies have relocated aspects of their data processing to India, and that their savings are now recorded on computer in that country. In addition, Indian software writers are regularly employed as subcontractors, and they keep in daily touch with the western world by fax and 'on line' data links.

The following advertisement appeared in the Spring 1995 edition of *Profiles* magazine. *Profiles* is the 'in house' magazine of the fourth-generation language company, Progress Software, quoted on the New York Stock Exchange.

Your search for progress development services ends here in India
The country with one of the largest reservoirs of software professionals in the world. With perhaps the most easily available and cost effective development services, using the latest technology. That's India. One of the largest Indian industrial houses brings to you PROGRESS consultancy services. A pool of brilliant computer professionals to take care of your software needs. We provide on site, off shore and turnkey software development services to fit your requirements. So if you want to avail the best which won't cost you the earth, just get in touch.

Another dilemma that international trade poses for the richer economies is that of the engineering company mentioned in chapter 6. The company that has sales per employee of only £25,000 per annum is still under constant pressure from its owners to improve profitability, and it clearly does not represent the sort of company that is going to allow the living standards of its workforce to rise much in the future. Therefore, should we try to retain this type of manufacturing and the employment that it represents, or should we be indifferent to its fate, and see it relocated to a low-wage area where the owners can raise their profits at the expense of wages?

The problem is not just one facing Europeans. There is a fierce debate taking place in America on the signing of the North American Free Trade Agreement (NAFTA). A series of stark examples are quoted by Ross Perot.[8]

In order to exploit the NAFTA agreement, the largest investment bank in Mexico and a group of Wall Street investors issued a prospectus to set up a company. The prospectus contained the following information. The company planned to buy US companies that are labor intensive and marginally profitable. Consequently the stock of these companies could be purchased at a very attractive price. The companies' manufacturing operations could then be relocated to Mexico to take advantage of the reduced labour costs. To quote directly from the prospectus

> We estimate that manufacturing companies that experience fully loaded gross labor costs in the $7–$10 range in the US may be able to utilise labor in Mexico at a fully loaded gross labor cost of $1.15 to $1.50 an hour... This could translate into annual savings of $10,000 to $17,000 per employee, creating a dramatic increase in profitability.

Potential investors were invited to invest in the company on the basis of buying the stock cheap and then selling it back to the market at a much higher price, on the back of increased profits made possible by subsistence-level Mexican wages. United States companies meeting the above criteria employ 5.8 million people. The answer to the question about keeping or losing this type of work has to be that the rich world must retain even these low-prospect jobs, until something better can be put in place. It has to be something better, otherwise we are making a fool's bargain and, as a society, selling a dollar for fifty cents.

It may suit the profit seekers to cherry pick what industries and related jobs they invest in and where they invest in them, but it suits no-one else. In a civilized country, people put out of work inevitably become a charge on the state. An economy growing at 3 per cent per year can barely re-absorb the people made redundant by technology. A wholesale rush to switch jobs to low-wage areas will swamp any economy and land the taxpayer with a burden that will be difficult to carry.

12

The Weird and Wonderful World of International Finance

The question therefore arises as to where the profits of all this low-cost or more efficient production are going if they are not going to increase the numbers of consumers or quality of consumers (in terms of increasing the amount of money they have to spend). Given the dismal investment record of most western economies when compared to their Pacific counterparts, particularly in the areas of industrial investment, they are not being applied to securing the future prosperity of those economies.

Japan does invest heavily in its own economy, but even after that it still generates huge quantities of 'surplus' funds. Kenichi Ohmae points out that in Japan, for example, private savings and the corporate sector generate more than $1 billion in surplus capital every day . . .

> . . . that has to be invested somewhere. Real consumption in more plants, more equipment can absorb only so much and virtually all of that can be financed with the cash flow generated by the depreciation of past capital investments.[1]

The answer is that some of the cash, and potentially a lot of the cash, is finding its way into a new trading economy that already dwarfs anything that has gone before, and would be beyond the imagination of Adam Smith and his successor free market economic thinkers. This is the economy of money. It is as far removed from the lives of ordinary people as if it was on the other side of the moon. It is also just as far removed from the control of national governments. It is a new global economy made possible in the last twenty years by the technologies of the computer and high-speed telecommunications. It also has the potential to starve the real world of the investment it needs to provide for future prosperity.

The total value of the output of all the world's nations is in the region of $25 trillion a year. If as much as one third of that is traded between nations in the exchange of raw materials and finished goods, then the value of world trade can be estimated at just over $8 trillion. Divided by 365 days in a year this approximates to $22 billion of trade a day. However, in 1993, every day an estimated $800 billion were traded across the world's foreign exchanges.[2] In 1994 the City of London claimed that it was handling $400 billion a day of this trade or 40 per cent of the world total.[3] If this is correct, then daily trading activity has grown to $1 trillion, a growth rate of 25 per cent per annum. What are the surplus $978 billion doing? Where did they all come from?

This is money being traded for its own sake and at the same time adding its own distortion which works against the best interests of the western nations. Dealers buy and sell the currencies that they feel confident with, and mark down currency in which they have less confidence. Fair enough from that point of view. However, this tends to undervalue the currency of emerging nations who have not as yet joined the club of 'accepted' money. Foreign exchange dealers will not be criticized so much by their managers for holding funds in the reserve currencies of dollars or yen as they would if they were holding the same amounts in Chinese yuan or Botswana's pula. However, between 1985 and 1992 Botswana was the fourth fastest growing economy in the world at 7.5 per cent per annum, just behind those of Thailand (8.6 per cent), South Korea (8.9 per cent) and China (9.2 per cent).

This marking down of currencies from emerging nations undervalues their exports and allows easier import penetration into western markets. Certainly standards of living are lower in the emerging economies, but can someone really live off $1 a day? Just to preserve life and limb, a Chinese worker needs 2,500 calories a day and a place to sleep just like any other human being. If that represents three bowls of rice a day and a lodging room, that cannot be had in any Western country for $1 a day. Maybe $5 or $10 might buy it. It takes just as much energy to melt steel in China as it does in America, so why should Chinese steel be cheaper, unless it is produced with intrinsically cheaper hydroelectricity? If comparisons between the costs of production in various economies were made on this basis, then not as many Western jobs would be at risk. Differences would still exist, but they would not be as great.

The total value of all the goods and services produced in the USA every year is approximately $5 trillion. Every day approximately $2 trillion are traded on Wall Street and in New York's other financial institutions.

In three days enough money has changed hands between the money men of New York to buy the entire annual output of the USA, the world's largest economy. The picture is just the same in London, Frankfurt or Tokyo. The economy of money is between 20 and 50 times larger than the real economy that rules the lives of ordinary people, according to Kurtzman,[2] and the economy of money is outside the control of all the central banks and other regulators. It is making up its own rules as it evolves. This may come as a surprise, but stop and think about it. It means that whatever the requirements of the ordinary citizen might be, as expressed through his spending power, they can be swamped by the imperatives driving this new economy. Speculators can bet billions against a currency in the certain knowledge that national governments cannot match the funds at their disposal. In so doing, they can drive up interest rates in the target economy and destroy the prosperity of ordinary families, who see the cost of home loans rise to unaffordable levels, and businesses find that the cost of money for investing is just too high for the returns available.

This money economy has several advantages over a traditional economy when it comes to making profits. In the first place nothing has to be made physically. No investment has to be committed to buildings, plant and machinery that can take several unproductive years to bring on stream. Nothing has to be transported to market, and once there, nothing has to be sold. From the moment it is created, money is ready to go to work in the money economy and, in skilful hands, earn profits. It can be traded once a month or once a week or several times a day. What is more the profits (or losses) are instantaneous and can be transmitted to the winner immediately over electronic networks. One or two people can control hundreds of millions of dollars or other currency equivalents. Several thousands of people would be involved with goods and services worth that sort of money in the physical economy that most people inhabit.

Historically the creation of money was the prerogative of government, and today governments still see themselves as the guardians of sound money. But the world has moved on and the new system now creates its own money. The oldest part of the money economy, the banks, have always been able to create money. They did so by printing their own bank notes which were backed up by a smaller value of gold held in reserve. This is where the saying 'a licence to print money' comes from. The abuse of this facility which triggered several runs on the banks in the nineteenth century led to the government-controlled central banks awarding themselves a monopoly to print bank notes. However, banks were still able to create money through the creation of credit and lending.

Money cascades through the banking system. One hundred pounds sterling, dollars or yen deposited with bank A allows that bank to lend out 88 per cent of that money to earn interest and to be able to pay interest to the depositor. The amount held back is a reserve to keep the bank liquid for day to day operations. The central banks dictate the amount of reserve required and can therefore control the extent by which a given amount of money can multiply through the system. The 88 per cent loaned will create another deposit in the same or another bank, and that in turn will be loaned out, less the reserve held back for safety reasons. This process continues until the final sum becomes too small to bother with. The amounts of reserve required by each central bank of the commercial banks operating in their jurisdictions varies, but the average effect of this cascade is to create eight times more money than was originally put into the system. In other words, governments are now only responsible for creating one eighth of the money supply, or less, when all the money instruments in circulation are taken into account.

Debt, and lots of it, has always been a vital part of the capitalist system, and if we all try to balance our books and live within our means this system will collapse. We have short-term savings, but usually choose to finance major purchases such as houses or cars. How far debt is ingrained in the system can be seen from the fact that, in this incestuous arrangement, the total gross debt that the US government and its citizens owe to each other and the outside world is estimated at $16 trillion, three times the annual GDP of the country. Indeed, it is governments themselves who can be the biggest borrowers of this privately created money.

The one good thing about all this new debt is that, on a temporary basis, it injects new spending power into an economy over and above the wages and salaries paid, and so keeps the system going a little longer. However, debt has to be repaid with interest. The consumer boom of the 1980s in the UK was fuelled by the ordinary citizen going into debt to historically high levels and speculating on property prices. The bust of the 1990s has been made more severe by the fact that that debt has had to be repaid. The prosperity was a fiction, though it did maintain jobs whilst it lasted.

Because banks have been around for a long time and have to have a physical presence in a country, they can be regulated, and central banks have developed an understanding of the basic tools of their trade such as credit and loans, etc. However, in the last thirty years the money markets have been deregulated and left to their own devices. In this period there has been invention and innovation, as there has been in all walks of life. New money instruments have been developed which even those working in the money industry can't keep track of. Some of the more common ones are futures, options, traded options, hedge funds, derivatives and the like. The total turnover of the new financial instruments now exceeds $140 trillion a year,[4] nearly six times the value of all the real activity in all the real economies of the world. There has also been an explosion in plastic money such as credit cards. Credit is money and the companies who issue credit cards increase the purchasing power of the population. Hundreds of billions of pounds worth of extra spending power has been released into the economies of the world by the issuing of credit cards and none of it is under the control of any central regulator.

Speed is also money. A bank note hoarded under a mattress may as well not exist. A bank note that passes through ten people's hands and facilitates ten transactions does twice as much work as a bank note that only passes through five people's hands. Whatever real money originally set this new money economy in motion, its value has been added to and increased out of all comprehension by the speed at which it is used. Today nothing is faster than the way a computer processes financial transactions. In a millionth of a second a billion dollars can leave New York and turn up in Tokyo or London. Just as quickly that money can do its work and move on to Paris or Cape Town. The new economy of money is an electronic economy, made up of a growing network of computers that has no concept of national boundaries. Regulators have as much chance of controlling it as they have of carrying water in a bucket full of holes. The network does not even control itself because it has no centre. It is a network of high-speed highways down which electronic bundles of money can pass at the touch of a button. Single transactions on the network can involve more money than the value of some small countries' output of goods for a whole year in the physical economy of the real world. If you think the situation is confusing you are right, because it is. Nobody today knows how much money there is in the world because nobody knows what money is any more. The electronic traders can recognize it when they see it but the man on the street has no idea.

To appreciate the complexity and novelty of what is happening it is worth looking in more detail at the evolving market in derivatives. I asked a contact working in this area of 'banking' to describe to me one of these new derivatives. They responded by saying 'Let's make one up'. Yes, make one up, because that is how things are evolving at the leading edge of this speculative finance. In this frontier land where dealers in their twenties can earn themselves millions, both the wise man and the reckless man can prosper, because there are no rules except that you must make a profit. The scenario goes something like this.

A creditworthy UK organization wants to raise a few hundred million pounds sterling, and a cash-rich German insurance company wants a home for the same amount of money. To avoid financial regulation in either the UK or Germany, the advising investment banker recommends that the bond be denominated in Japanese yen. For good measure the bond is made optionally convertible from yen into French francs, in the unlikely event that the Japanese authorities decide to take an interest in what is going on. A truly international and unregulated financial instrument has now been created.

At a future date the German insurance company decides that the long-term prospects for the yen are not as good as might be the case for the US dollar, and wishes to cash out of the yen bond and buy into a dollar bond instead. A friendly investment bank is always on hand to advise, especially if they think that the German insurer has misread the market. They therefore buy the bonds off the German insurer with a mind to sell them on to another client.

However, the new client only likes the capital part of the yen bond, particularly as it was issued at an attractive discount to its maturity value, i.e. issued at, say, 80 per cent of its face value at par. He therefore negotiates a price for the capital component of the bond and buys it in a new contract with the investment bank.

The investment bank now has an interest flow of yen for the next several years to sell to clear its books. It knows another client who will buy the interest flow, but on its own the deal is not big enough for him. The investment bank can oblige because from another deal they have an unbundled interest flow in dollars that will make up the difference. These two are combined to make a new financial instrument, or derivative, which is duly sold.

None of this financial engineering is anything to do with the UK institution which originally raised money through a bond issue. All it is legally obliged to do is to pay the monies contracted for to the German insurer. The German insurer has to pass them on to the investment bank, who in turn has to split them up appropriate to the new financial instrument that it has created, and pay them on to the people who have purchased the new instruments.

The life of these bonds can be twenty years or more, so in that time they can be sold on, dismantled, re-combined, etc. many times according to the different views people take of the market as events unfold. Each player in the chain has to pass the parcels of monies along until they reach the current, ultimate owner, whoever that might be.

Complicated? Yes, this example is one of the more complex ones, but this complexity and the natural volatility of the markets introduces the opportunity to make huge profits if you can gamble the markets and win, particularly if your gambles are leveraged via options as so many hedge funds are.

Risky? Yes, because each link in the chain is a separate contract, often involving hundreds of millions in currency. If any link in the chain goes bust or defaults in any way the next link will have to finance the loss. Given the size of the accumulated trades, any default by a major institution has the potential to destabilize the entire banking system.

Why are the banks doing this type of business when most people would see the role of banks as being one of helping to finance industry and commerce, or of helping the man in the street to buy a family house? The answer is simple – profit. As a leading investment banker, interviewed in the *Financial Times*, put it,

> I invite anyone to point to a fee that's gone up in the last 10 years. Fees only decline. If adequate returns on capital are to be maintained, it will be a trading world.[5]

This might have been true in the 1980s, but since then British banks at least have found new ways of making money. They now charge ordinary customers and small businesses for everything that they can. There are even reports of bank managers being taken out for lunch by their customers as a pleasant, informal way of discussing business and then later sending their hosts a large bill for their time. The major British banks are currently showing profits running into billions of pounds sterling a year, with Barclays as the top earner at nearly £2 billion for 1994.

British banks now have so much profit that they are finding it difficult to find safe ways of investing it. As funding new business start-ups and small businesses in general is deemed to be too risky, one authority at the Bank of England is reported to have suggested that they should use their profits to buy back some of their own shares. This would reward the shareholders and drive up the value of their remaining shares in the market. What ever happened to the idea that banks should use their funds to promote industry and commerce?

The question therefore arises as to whether it matters if the banks and the financial markets are inventing new ways to make money out of guessing the future values of the new financial instruments that they are creating. The answer is that it probably does matter and it might matter a lot. Firstly, there is the impact that these new activities may be having in changing the focus of the banking system. Two examples taken from the *Financial Times* make the point.[6] Between 1989 and 1993 the traditional loan book of the Bankers Trust fell from $18.4 billion to $13.9

billion, whilst trading in financial instruments rose from $12.2 billion to $48.3 billion and the total accumulated exposure to derivatives rose to $1,923 billion. The story at J. P. Morgan is much the same. In the last five years its traditional loan book has fallen from $26 billion to $23.2 billion whilst its trading activities have risen from $89 billion to $134 billion and its total exposure to derivatives now stands at $1,731 billion. Other banks are following the profits and doing the same.

The second reason why it matters is just the sheer size of the exposures that this activity is creating. At $1,923 billion the exposure of just one bank is approaching half the value of the entire output of the US economy for a whole year. If something unimaginable happened to cause a catastrophic collapse of one of these financial institutions, the effect would be like a hydrogen bomb exploding in the heart of the world's financial system, and the fallout would be devastating.

When something as potentially profitable as trading or gambling in derivatives happens on the scene, it inevitably entices other, less experienced, players into the game. Ordinary commercial enterprises, anxious to squeeze every ounce of profit from their assets, are considering making their treasury departments into separate profit centres. Some already have and some have already suffered serious losses. The following are three instances that have come to light recently. Kashima Oil of Japan has lost $1.5 billion, Metallgesellschaft of Germany has lost $1.4 billion and Proctor and Gamble has lost $102 million. All were trading in derivatives, when their main business has traditionally been to produce real things in the real world for real people.

Since I first wrote the above there have been even more spectacular casualties. Orange County in California is a case in point. However, the biggest surprise is that of the Barings Bank in London. Fortunately this was only a small bank, but nevertheless it should act as a warning to everyone of what can happen, and we should be grateful that it was 'only' a small bank. However, what business does any bank have in betting on which way the Nikkei index will go? Who actually cares which way it goes? It can only go up or down, the odds are 50/50. These are the same odds as you get playing black or red on the roulette tables in Las Vegas. This is large-scale gambling, plain and simple. It adds not a jot to the economic well-being of the man in the street and it ties up vast quantities of capital that should be better applied to things that matter.

The one thing about electronic gadgetry is that it gets cheaper by the month. At one time investors had to go through a stock broker or banker to gain access to shares and investments. Today all they need is a satellite dish, a personal computer, an account clearance and they can become part of this electronic trading network from anywhere in the world. The easier it gets, the more savings and wealth are diverted into it. The more savings and wealth that go into this network, the less likely they are to be applied in the communities in which they were generated. They are more likely to be applied to speculation for quick profit than to be invested at all. The world is in danger of being sucked into a destructive spiral.

The problem the electronic traders are creating is this. The new system is attracting away from the real world money that should and could be used for real investment. It is a sort of modern equivalent of the hoarding. It is also creating its own supply of money by its inventiveness at creating new money instruments and by the velocity at which it uses traditional money funds. There is now more money in this electronic money economy than there are goods and services in the real economy. Massive speculation can wreck the economic policies of elected governments. From time to time large chunks of this money can descend into the real world. In the 1980s traders used to talk of 'walls of money' descending on to the markets. This is the classic cause of inflation, i.e. 'too much money chasing too few goods'. On balance this hot money does not like investing in start-up schemes when it can invest in existing enterprises or assets with proven track records. Thus inflation takes place on the stock exchanges of the world as the surplus money bids up the prices of existing stocks and shares. This can also filter down to other assets such as property, both commercial offices and private houses. It can also give an unhelpful twist to wage inflation as people working in financial markets see their earnings rise rapidly to several times that of equivalent professionals. The sizes of these bonuses are staggering. When the ING Bank rescued Barings Bank from total collapse it set aside £100 million to honour staff bonuses. Even in failure the system looks after its own.

Rising prices for existing assets encourage more money to be invested in them, thus increasing the upward pressure on their prices well before the real economy can respond with increased supply. This introduces inflation into the economy which the government sees as its duty to control. The only tool that most governments have for the task is the ability to raise interest rates. This bears down heavily on the man in the street who is not really the cause of the problem, and it discourages investment which would help to solve the problem. On the other hand, it rewards the money that originally caused the problem, by paying it a higher rate of return in the form of higher interest to sit in bank accounts and do nothing. Investment in the creation of real wealth, that would narrow the gap between the growing amount of new money and the inadequate stock of real assets that the money is supposed to represent, is discouraged.

Inflation is now endemic in most advanced economies. Governments today try to act responsibly in the creation of traditional money by not printing too much of it and, where they can, restricting the availability of credit through the banking system. However, the more the new money economy acts irresponsibly, the stricter governments have to become with the creation of traditional money to keep the situation under control. To achieve zero inflation draconian measures of deflation are required. In fact, some economists and policy makers have become obsessed with the control of inflation as the touchstone of sound economic thinking. When Alan S. Blinder, a Keynesian-inclined member of the Federal Reserve Board, suggested that unemployment as well as inflation was the concern of central banks, he was roundly condemned by monetarist economists as being too soft for the job.[7] The British Chancellor of the day, Norman Lamont, used this sentiment when describing his anti-inflation policy, 'If it's not hurting, it's not working'. However this is where traditional economic theory breaks down. It has never before had to face a situation like this and its traditional ideas, monetarist or other, though comforting in the way old dictums tend to be, are part of the problem instead of being part of the solution.

Investment is needed in the real economy but it is more profitable to make it in the money economy. The activities and needs of the money economy now influence, if not drive, interest rate policies. The amount of money that banks, particularly the international banks and their dealing subsidiaries, are investing in computer technology to gamble in this market, rivals the amount of investment manufacturing industry can afford to make, to produce real things. Banks and other financial institutions don't create anything that people can wear or eat. Their original purpose was to act on behalf of companies operating in the real economy. Now they are helping to divert resources away from that economy into an electronic world where only a few can benefit. No one seems to know the damage they are doing. They are just following the lure of short-term profits, and profit, even if it is only on paper, is now the only measure of success.

13

The Paradigm Shift

The new technology that is becoming available has two aspects to it. On the one hand its power has the ability to deliver prosperity and leisure to everyone, and on the other hand it gives people who are focused on profit, and the accumulation of wealth, more powerful tools which they can use to control more of the world's wealth for themselves. In the past, monarchs fought each other for control of territory. The battleground has now transferred to the board room. Today, captains of industry fight each other for global market share. They, like the princes before them, are not overly concerned for the fortunes of the foot soldiers. Workers are just expensive numbers when the most important number is the bottom line profit. To win is to survive to fight another battle, and each battle creates its own winners and its own wasteland.

However, we know from our own experience that human society is not just composed of combative people. In fact the majority of folk are not competitive in this way. They would prefer co-operation. They want a better life for themselves and their families and they are prepared to work for it. But a better life is not just money in the bank, welcome though that is. A better life is also about the time to enjoy life. It is about the quality of life, and they would prefer not to have to achieve it at someone else's expense. Progress to the majority of people is better if it means progress for everyone. They know what the combative captains of industry have failed to grasp, and that is that in the long term they, the ordinary people, are needed as consumers even if they are not needed as workers. Where will the profits come from if no one can buy the output of the super-efficient factories because everyone has been automated out of a job? We are not just individuals, we are part of a system.

Thus we have a dilemma. On the one hand the message, handed down from the top by a minority, is that we must play their game and compete to survive. In today's world, with today's advances, that means employing fewer people and more technology and working both harder. On the other hand the only means that most people have of gaining a share of the good life is through having a job, and a job that pays well. This is supposed to make us uncompetitive. The dilemma must be solved unless we are prepared to see the re-emergence of a society in which the few aggregate everything to themselves and the majority are left with nothing.

The danger is there to be seen in other areas of life too. By bringing the wrong mindset to a situation we run the risk of doing tremendous damage. Is the care of sick people compatible with the profit motive? Commercial, competitive accounting practices have evolved as a way, possibly the best way to date, of directing the affairs of companies. Their fundamental logic is designed to maximize profit, as a percentage return on capital, by containing activity within predefined costs and then seeking to minimize those costs. They collect the information in a way that supports this type of decision making. However, with health care, for example, we have tremendous potential within the community to train doctors and nurses and provide the other facilities that could deliver maximum health care to anyone who needs it, and not just those who can pay for it. However, the commercial accounting approach will lead people down other paths of thought. For example if 100 people are being treated in two hospitals it might suggest that if one of the hospitals were to be closed, then ninety people could be treated in the remaining hospital for 80 per cent of the previous cost. People susceptible to this logic would then be encouraged to make the obvious choice, and 10 per cent of the population who could have been treated will not be treated because it is uneconomic to do so.

In Britain we have a National Health Service that, by non-monetary criteria, serves the population well. It delivers care, when it is needed, free of charge to the patient. In recent times this service has been the subject of an experiment, whereby market forces and financial measurements have been introduced in an attempt to make it more efficient. It turns out that a doctor who was an adviser to the government and one of the principal architects of the reforms was himself addicted to the drug heroin. The doctor has since been prosecuted and received a suspended prison sentence. However, what is more revealing is the help that the drug gave him in forming his opinions.

The doctor did not believe heroin affected his clinical judgement. . . .
However, he believes the drug made him much more ruthless and less
compassionate as to the effects the health service reforms would have on
patients.[1]

In the doctor's own words:

I believed that management and finances were much more important than
the lot of the individual patient. Heroin enabled me to put the patients
aside and concentrate on getting the financial structures correct, which I
believed would ultimately be for the good of the patients. I was detached.

Our thought processes have been hi-jacked by the idea that we have to
monetarize everything and that everything can have a monetary value
attached to it. Profit-oriented competition is being introduced into health
care, education, the allocation of resources to old people, and into all
aspects of society that were previously served by different criteria. It is
only necessary to look in the management section of a bookshop. There
are books on how to beat the competition, how to sell to win, how to
get more out of the workforce, how to survive in a competitive environment, how to get rich quickly. The language that they employ is the
language of combat. Co-operation and sharing hardly get a look in. You
are what you can grab for yourself, even if it would make more sense to
do otherwise.

There are real problems, and there are problems of our own making,
which evaporate when we realize that we have simply been looking at
the world the wrong way round. Society is going to continue to evolve
and it is wrong that evolution will be allowed to take us backwards in
terms of economic well-being. The fact that there is a severe danger that
living standards will fall is due to our hanging on to the ideas of the past
or applying the wrong measurements to guide our thoughts. The real
remedy lies in a new understanding of what is developing, and seeing
how it can be turned to advantage. In scientific jargon, a paradigm shift,
a completely new way of looking at the world.[2]

Charles Handy, in *The Future of Work*,[3] talks of the 80 per cent and
the 20 per cent split. The 80 per cent of the population want continuity,
they see problems as temporary phenomena capable of solution by short-
term measures and quick fixes. They seek confirmation and comfort in
the opinions of like-minded people, newspapers and politicians. They
take refuge in group thinking that seeks to exclude the opinions of those
who hold dissenting views. So long as they are right they provide stability and continuity to society, and prevent society from disintegrating

under the weight of irreconcilable and competing minority viewpoints. However, it is of critical importance to decide if things really are changing because, if they are, then this holding of a steady course is sailing the ship of state straight on to the rocks. There have been many times in the past when the majority has been wrong. In fact all change, by definition, is originated by a minority.

Until the telescope was invented people's factual knowledge of the sky was limited. All sorts of fanciful stories were invented, usually around the activities of gods, to explain the motion of the planets and the stars. The Christian Church in particular chose to believe and enforce the belief that everything revolved around the earth. When Copernicus challenged the idea, and asserted that everything revolved around the sun, this new heresy was fiercely resisted although the facts supported it. Eventually the Church had to capitulate, and there was a paradigm shift in our understanding of the heavens, and the science of astronomy was able to proceed to the next stage in its evolution.

Europeans used to believe that the earth was flat. The logical reasoning from this belief was that if you travelled far enough in any one direction you would eventually come to an edge and fall off into an unknown hell. Early maps showed these regions populated by strange monsters. So strong was this belief that early explorers stayed within sight of land wherever possible. Merchants would not put up the money for the exploration of deep sea routes to other lands, even though there was no hard evidence that danger existed. It was enough that the danger existed in men's imaginations. It was not until Christopher Columbus sailed out into the Atlantic and discovered America that European minds were freed from this restriction. The resulting exploration, activity and colonization has, for good or bad, shaped the history of the planet ever since.

The concept of the paradigm shift is a scientific one, and science contains many examples of it in action. It used to be believed that disease occurred spontaneously. Because medical thinkers did not have access to microscopes they could not see the tiny organisms that caused diseases, so they reasoned that disease occurred spontaneously out of nowhere. Some people even speculated that it was a form of divine retribution for sin. As a result, they did not think to look for cures in the areas where they would be most likely to find them, and instead had to concentrate on treating the symptoms of the diseases. In particular they had no idea that disease could be spread from patient to patient on the hands of a doctor or the unwashed knives that were used by them in operations. Hospitals were the most dangerous places in which to be ill and no one knew why.

Louis Pasteur, working on the reason why wine could go sour, discovered that micro-organisms invisible to the naked eye were the cause of his problem. It did not take him long to make the connection between his discovery and the transmission of disease, and from that how important sterilization, cleanliness and general hygiene were in medical terms. This was such a profound challenge to accepted thought that the medical establishment fiercely resisted his new ideas. It was also an embarrassment for proud men to admit that they had been wrong and, in their collective mistake, had caused the loss of countless lives. Thankfully the establishment did not prevail and millions of us owe our lives to this change in thinking. The world did not change, only our way of thinking about it.

There are many more examples of pioneering, some would say maverick, free thinkers who have thought the unthinkable or even the seemingly ridiculous, and triumphed to the ultimate benefit of us all. Where would we be without Darwin's contribution to natural history or Einstein's contribution to physics? The one thing all new ideas have shared in common is the hostility of those people whose beliefs they have upset, because changing just one belief can force on to people a completely new world view, and that is a very disturbing experience. People will hold on to old, even outmoded, beliefs just to avoid this experience. The more deeply held the belief, the more difficult it is to change; it can become an article of faith.

Indeed, anybody could have made the simple connection between medical staff not washing their hands or surgical implements and the spreading of disease, but they did not until Louis Pasteur came at the problem from a slightly different angle. This is because once an idea has taken hold it seems to set about destroying or excluding its competitors. If disease occurs spontaneously then there is no point in being clean in the practice of medicine. If the earth is flat then there is no point in sailing out into danger. If progress can only be made through competitive advantage, and that can only be achieved by employing new technology and fewer people, then why look for other ways to solve the problem? At least that is what some people would like us to believe. When an idea has taken hold it can be very difficult to dislodge, and human thought is set on tracks that can lead in the right or wrong direction.

What paradigm or mindset are we employing when we look at today's challenges and is it still relevant? Indeed is it one that we have freely chosen for ourselves or is it one that others have subtly imposed upon us?

If we choose to limit our vision and look at everything through the eyes of money then we will, of course, remain obsessed with thoughts of having to pay for everything. It is worth remembering that the traditional economic justification of the role of money has been to ration, restrict and prioritize scarce resources amongst competing needs. It is inappropriate to apply this treatment to naturally abundant resources or goods that can be produced in abundance by robotized production facilities. If it is forced into these situations, then all that money will do is try to ration and restrict that which does not need rationing or restricting with the perverse effect of creating scarcity where none need exist. The system has to do this for its own survival. Traditional economics cannot exist without prices and prices cannot exist without some form of scarcity.

If we are going to survive as a cohesive society in a world where machines do the work, then we are going to have to re-think our ideas in some fundamental ways, particularly with respect to money, ownership and social responsibility.

Certainly the role of money will have to be diminished. It took one hundred years for the British economy to be transformed from agricultural to industrial. Over the next fifty years the transformation will be from a work-based economy to a consumer-based economy in a new sense of the word. Most of the basics that we need to sustain a tolerable standard of living will be produced for us automatically without the need for human intervention. Robots will make what we need and robots will make and maintain the robots that make what we need. This is a fundamental challenge to the way our present economic theories tell us to behave. These theories state that what can't be paid for is a surplus, and that surplus must be cut back until there is a shortage sufficient to command a price in the market place and an opportunity for profit. In other words, traditional economics will try to prevent a truly prosperous future happening for the workless majority of mankind. Only those people with money or access to money through employment can offer a price for products. Traditional economics will collapse the system back from supplying everyone to supplying the dwindling core of people who have not yet been replaced by more efficient robots. Say's law, which states that supply creates its own balancing demand, and on which many conservative economists and politicians base their supply side policies, will no longer apply because this production will be outside the human economy. Products, both goods and services, created by robots will have to be free because they will be free. There will be no real costs associated with their production. No human hands will have laboured to create them and no human wages will have been paid to bestow a value upon them. They will just be there if they are allowed to be.

The first technology to make it past the finishing line will be in place for a very long time, and will only be ousted on environmental or health or safety criteria. You can't get more efficient than free. There will be no need to put in any further investment because the system will have become self-sustaining. It will be like a young person leaving home to set up life on their own, after the parents have invested years of resources on their behalf. However with sums of money of this magnitude involved, the leave-taking will not be without problems, the parents may not want to let go.

The transition of assets from the private sector to the community will not be easy. The assets could be essentially worthless because they will not, in a competitive situation, be able to earn any return. The pressure will be on the owners to maintain or create an artificial shortage and to exploit it. They will claim their natural rights as owners to do with their property what they wish. However, their position will become increasingly untenable the longer a fully automatic system is in place, and the links with the real investment that created it are weakened by the passage of time. Nevertheless no-one gives up important positions of power without a struggle. Wars have been fought over land and revolutions have overturned exploitative economic systems. In these circumstances everyone loses. A smooth transition to the inevitable will be in everyone's best interests.

Eventually sector after sector of the fundamental economy will drop out of the realms of conventional economics and become just another natural resource to be enjoyed by mankind. They will become like the free air we breathe or the clean water that we drink. We will need to take the same care of them as we are learning to take with these truly natural resources.

Ownership does have its advantages. If something is owned then the owner, or owners, can be responsible for looking after the asset. However if there is no clear ownership then it is highly likely that the asset will be neglected and, if abused, fall into disrepair. We can see this from the way public property is treated by vandals. We can see it from the way that whole species have been hunted to extinction, and fisheries in international waters have been over-fished to the point of no return for the fish stocks. In these circumstances a sense of responsibility has to be imposed on the exploiters by the community. In the first instance the local community has to act and in the second instance the international community has to act. In the future many of our economic assets will have to be similarly protected. The principles of the Green Movement and environmentalists in general that encourage us to act responsibly towards the environment, will also be applicable towards our fully robotized productive assets.

There will always be a leading edge where individuals of a certain talent can make a contribution to society and their own wealth at the same time. The economics of the future will need them just as they are needed today, and they should be encouraged in what they do best. We need to retain the ability for creative destruction but we need to contain and minimize the scope of competitive destruction.

However, there is a place for entrepreneurial frontier economics, and that is at the frontier. Its abrasive, confrontational, and competitive style is suited to uncharted and unclaimed territories. It is not suited to settled and well-serviced areas of society where the best message is 'If it ain't broke don't fix it'. Once goods and services are capable of being supplied automatically without human intervention, then they become off limits to competitive, destructive economics.

Having a frontier or leading edge implies that there is also a trailing edge. At the leading edge there will be a high level of human input. At the trailing edge there will be a low or non-existent level of human input. As the economy progresses, these two edges will move forward, leaving a trail of activities that have passed through both edges. The length of time an activity remains between these two edges will depend on the pace of its technical change. As a technology enters the leading edge it will be the subject of competitive economic activity, as it makes room for itself by elbowing something else out of the way. If it survives and matures it will ultimately pass out of the trailing edge into the realm of free goods there to be used by all.

Between the leading edge and the trailing edge there should be plenty of room for the 15 per cent or so of the people who want to be defined by the work they do and the wealth that they accumulate for themselves.

Finally, let us once again make use of our imaginations. Using our imaginations is the most effective way of seeing existing facts in a new light, and it is about the only way of predicting the future. Imagine a tropical island paradise where a perfect climate and fertile soil ensures that food grows naturally. All the inhabitants have to do is reach out and pick whatever they want to eat. The warm, shallow sea around the coast is similarly productive. A fishing line lowered into the water will always yield a catch within minutes. In other words, the lucky inhabitants have all their physical requirements provided by nature. Poverty and hunger are unknown to them. Now imagine that a black ship sails into the bay and the island is claimed as part of an empire.

Imagine that the crew of the ship have come from a part of the world where the climate is less favourable. A part of the world where there are long, hard winters and life has always been a constant battle for survival. Under these conditions their society has developed a work ethic that is harsh but essential. The ethic is, that if you do not work then you do not deserve to eat because you are making yourself into a burden that other people have to carry. Everything has to be won from nature so everything is owned by the person who put the work in. Indeed the ethic has such force that it has come to mean that if you take something that you have not worked for, then you are in fact stealing that item because it must belong to someone else who put in the work.

The easy life that the crew find the native population enjoying offends their sense of right and wrong which, after several generations, has become deeply ingrained into their culture. As conquerors, they feel that they have the duty and the right to impose their moral standards on the natives and so they set about enforcing the work ethic. To prevent the natives from stealing food, all the natural plantations and groves where the food crops grow are fenced off. The natives are told that they can only eat if they pay for what they require, and that they can get the money to pay by working.

The only work available is strictly limited. The food grows naturally so there is no work there. The new masters, however, require servants and the food areas need guarding to prevent theft. Whilst the lucky few are performing these duties they can't be fishing or mending their houses, thus there arises some secondary employment for a few other natives performing these duties. However, the majority of the population are fenced out and can only scratch a desperate living in any way that they can. There is still enough food to feed everyone but that would involve giving it away free, which would destroy its price and upset the market-based economy. Instead the new masters leave the surplus to rot and for the following year lay plans to take the surplus acreage out of production and turn it over to some other use.

A paradise such as this will rarely have existed except in the minds of poets and storytellers. Paradise lost is a common and attractive theme. However we are not looking to the past; we are looking to the future. We are not depending on the whims of mother nature and the weather to provide the perfect environment. We are looking to our technology to do the job and, properly handled, the emerging technology is going to be more reliable than nature in this respect. The challenge for us is threefold. Firstly, whether we can even comprehend a world in which science and technology deliver the goods without us having to work for them in the ways we have become used to. Secondly, whether we are prepared to do what is necessary to bring about such a world for everyone. Thirdly, if we are not prepared to channel science and technology in this direction, dare we imagine what other type of world we might create with it? The technology stands ready to be used in any way we choose, but how do we stand?

14

The Future

=====

The unknown and unpredictable can be frightening things. Nevertheless it is important to try to look into the crystal ball and describe events that are reasonably certain to happen. To be forewarned is to be forearmed. What follows is not a comprehensive description of the future, only a small selection of important trends that can be extrapolated from the way today's technology is unfolding. In the final analysis, people will make the future by using technology wisely or foolishly.

Computers

The star of the electronics world is undoubtedly the computer. It started out as a roomful of clumsy electronic circuitry in Manchester University in 1948, and through the technology of micro-miniaturization has become the marvel that it is today. It will move on from here but the technology, even as it stands, is poised to make major impacts on our lives in the near future.

Modern computers work in this way. At their centre is a processing chip which need be no more than 1 cm square, about the size of a thumbnail and about the same thickness. On to this chip have been etched millions of electrical devices and millions of connections between these devices. This intricate circuitry allows numbers to be manipulated, and through yes/no logic it allows decisions to be made. Controlling the speed at which the chip operates is an electronic clock very similar to the quartz digital watches on sale in high street shops. Quartz crystals have the property that when they are excited by having a small current of electricity applied to them, they vibrate regularly and very quickly. Large crystals of pure quartz are artificially grown and are then cut into thin slices. These slices are then cut into circular pieces about the size of a contact lens. They are then ground down to the thickness necessary. The thinner they are the higher is the frequency at which they vibrate. Curvatures can be added for additional properties. The crystals in quartz watches are relatively imprecise because they have to be accurate only to the second. They cost only pennies. The higher-specification computer crystals have to be accurate to hundreds of millionths of a second and so cost a lot more.

Each vibration represents the opening of a gateway, through which a tiny pulse of electricity can start its journey along the circuits of the chip and perform one instruction. It is now common to have even small computers running at 100 MIPS. This means 100 million instructions per second. As is typical with this technology, dramatic improvements are in the pipeline. The next generation of computer chips will run ten times as fast and they are due for release in 1996. Digital Equipment, the second largest computer company in the world, has already announced its Alpha 21164 chip running at 1 billion instructions per second, and other manufacturers are about to follow suit. At these speeds and with appropriate software, these computers will be able to mimic the interactive way humans communicate with each other.

The developments do not end here. Scientists working at Cambridge University have just announced another breakthrough. With current technology the degree to which the etchings on the silicon chips can be miniaturized is a crucial determinant of the speed at which the chip can run. These scientists have discovered a practical way of reducing the etchings down to only ten molecules of width. It will take between five and ten years to turn the knowledge to actual use, but this development has the potential to multiply the speed at which computer chips work by 500 times.

Instructions in this context means machine-level instructions. A simple command like 'Find this information' may comprise 5,000 machine instructions, but this hardly matters when there are tens of millions available every second. Modern computer chips can easily support a hundred different users all asking for different things at the same time. The computer seems to be responding simultaneously, but it is really responding sequentially, at such a speed that it appears to be simultaneous.

Price is no longer a barrier to the spread of this technology. As the chips have got faster so mass production has made them cheaper. Table 14.1 illustrates the point.

Table 14.1 *Decreasing price of computer technology*

Date and type of computer	MIPS	Price
1975 Mainframe	10	$10,000,000
1976 Super Computer	160	$20,000,000
1979 First Mini Computer	1	$200,000
1981 First Personal Computer	0.25	$3,000
1994 Second Generation PCs	100	$3,000
1995 Superfast Video Game Box	1,000	$500

Information has to be fed into, and the finished results taken away from, the chip, and this is done through the random access memory or RAM. This is another silicon chip of about the same size as the processor chip but it has been etched in a different way. This chip stores information as a code of 'on or off' dots that spell out messages like Morse code. It works a little more slowly than the processing chip because, before any information can be pulled for processing, an index has to be referred to, to see where the information is stored.

The bottleneck that slows down today's computers occurs when information has to be read from, or written to, the hard disk. This is the only remaining mechanical part of the machine and is still used because it stores information permanently. It is the library of the computer holding permanently millions of pieces of information. When the computer is switched off the information in the chip-based random access memory is lost, but that on the disk is kept.

As a mechanical device, the read/write heads on a disk can manage only approximately thirty accesses per second. When compared to the millions of accesses per second possible with the solid-state random access memory, the drawbacks of mechanical technology are evident, and they slow down the speed at which a computer can operate.

Solid-state random access memories now exist that can replace the slower disks and they are in small-scale production. They do not lose their information when the power is switched off. When production of these solid-state replacements for moving disks is geared up for the mass market, today's most powerful computers will become no bigger that a centimetre cube. The price too will be that of a mass-produced commodity, maybe no more than a few dollars or pounds sterling each. Small and cheap, they will be able to be incorporated into almost any product to give it almost human capabilities. It can be fun to speculate. How about a pen that knew when you were spelling a word incorrectly, or a pen that could automatically transmit a fax of what you had just written? How about a washing machine that could adjust itself to the requirements of the clothes that it was washing? Some microwave ovens already have a computerized nose inside them to sniff when the food is cooked, and they can distinguish between meat and vegetables. How about a supervisor that could tirelessly and instantaneously run a factory of automatic machinery? Computers are already running large sectors of industry and commerce, where the complexity is such that it is beyond human ability to do the job. Some financial derivatives are already so fiendishly complex that they can only be valued by using the arithmetic skills of computers. In this respect the computers are making the buy and sell decisions that control billions' worth of currency. Programmed trading is said to have been one of the factors that contributed to the stock market crash of 1987. How about a dictation machine that can understand your voice, and automatically translate that into correctly spelt and punctuated text, on a page of paper ready to mail out to a business contact? This last item is not science fiction. This example is included because it is already a commercial product that you can purchase. It was developed by Dragon Systems in the USA, originally to help disabled people who could speak but who could not use their limbs. Now that fast computers are here it is available to anyone. Over the next few years it will completely alter the mix of skills in most offices. The highly efficient secretary typing letters and reports will not be needed in that role and one more major source of employment will come under pressure. The *Daily Mail* (1 June 1994) ran the following headline 'Computer that could talk typists out of a job'. It could come true sooner than we think.

There is another technology bottleneck that is holding back the more widespread use of computers. This is bandwidth. The amount of information computers process can be enormous. If they then have to pass that information along to another computer, the old style copper wires do not have the capacity to pass the information along quickly enough. What is needed is technology like fibre optics that can handle thousands of simultaneous messages in one threadlike strand. This is why billions of dollars are being invested in re-wiring whole countries with fibre optic super highways. Once these are in place, interactive video telephones will be practical. People will be able to work from home and be in visual contact with the other members of their workgroup. People will be able to control machines from hundreds of miles away. Doctors will be able to perform operations without being anywhere near their patients. People will be able to shop from home. The list of possibilities is endless, as are the social consequences that these developments will cause. Until now nation states could control their populations by regulating travel and censoring the information allowed in across the borders.

Tomorrow anyone with a receiver will have access to the whole world. What price frontiers then or for that matter national loyalty?

Computers are nothing if they are not programmed with instructions of what to do and how to react in given circumstances. Today programming is where the money is being made in the industry. The giant computer manufacturers are dismissing their factory workers, as they take their own medicine and apply computer technology to the manufacture of computers. Computer salespeople are being made redundant as the public becomes more knowledgeable and confident enough with the new technology to buy it off the shelf just like any other piece of hardware. The jobs in the industry are for people who can think of, write, and sell new software applications, and this is where another change is taking place.

Computer programming always used to be very logical, employing if/then reasoning. If this happens then do that. This approach assumes that the programmer can think up all the possible 'if this' situations and apply to them the correct 'do that' answers. Unfortunately everything in the world does not fit into this neat and finite way of doing things. Object-oriented programming is going to go some way towards solving this problem, but it is only a halfway solution. When something unpredictable happens, or when something that should not happen does happen, then all these types of computer programs crash or fall over or give out wrong answers. When this happens, people blame the machine and call it stupid, which in a way it is.

The biggest computer project failures occur regularly when people embark on grand projects that try to link everything into a computer through a mass of interwoven logic that contains hidden contradictions. Given our biology and limited ability to manipulate more than seven pieces of data at one time, we can't foresee all the outcomes of very complex situations, so we can't easily design and build systems that push us beyond these limits. One way we react to this is by closing down the options in a program to a number that we can handle. We write software which in essence says that if you want to use a computer then it has to be in this way only and for certain things only. This works well in many situations where we don't want people to have many choices, but in other situations it is narrowing and restrictive, giving people the impression that their creativity is being restrained by the narrow boundaries that the computer has been programmed to expect. All this is to change.

A new approach to programming computers is now feasible and it attempts to copy the way people go about problem solving. It is called neural computing. The term is borrowed from the medical profession where it is used to describe how the human brain functions. Instead of using the rigid 'If this then do that' approach to problem solving, it says 'If this then try that and remember the outcome and compare it to the result we would like to have'. Thus after a period of learning and comparing results, the less successful strategies can be abandoned. The data makes the rules. Humans learn in this way. The computer is able to learn and to change, because if the input data changes it can take this into account and modify its strategy to once again achieve the correct results.

This new form of computer programming is so important that the UK Department of Trade and Industry has set up a neural computing[1] campaign, with its own newsletter and information service on projects currently under way or actually completed. In the issue of April 1994, thirty-four areas of development are listed ranging from medical diagnosis to credit risk management. Ultimately, hardly any area of human activity will be untouched by this semi-intelligent learning software.

Systems such as these are now being used by financial firms to predict when to buy and sell shares. For a period of months the computers are taught by being fed information such as interest rate changes, exchange rate changes, market research predictions, and any other economic data, and they are asked to predict which shares to trade or which currencies to buy. Every time they make a correct prediction they are told of their success, and the particular neural pathways used in that selection are reinforced. Eventually their success rates rise to the level where they can be left to trade on their own. Computers do not mind working overnight, so this is where they have been applied first, trading on the overnight markets. Results so far show that these programmed traders outperform the market by 19 per cent. In other words, given £1 million to trade with, the computer will make a profit of £190,000 a year.

Neural network computing did not exist before 1988. In 1994 neural software achieved $500 million worth of sales. By 1998 it is predicted that the market will be in excess of $2 billion per year and growing rapidly.

When this neural computing is linked to 'fuzzy logic' the results can be surprising. Fuzzy logic is another up and coming development. One reason why artificial intelligence has been slow to evolve is because we have been applying the wrong scientific paradigm to it. Traditional science likes to ask specific questions and receive exact answers. Robots in science fiction make fun of the imprecise way humans communicate. However it is just this imprecision that underlies the comprehensive nature of human intelligence.

Humans, to take an example, talk to each other in the following way: 'I like to wear red clothes on cold days because it makes me feel warmer.'

A companion will immediately understand the sense of what is being said. A computer would not. Programmed according to traditional scientific paradigms, the computer will need precise definitions of red, cold, warm, etc. It will need to know when cold ceases and warm begins, when red ceases and purple begins. It will need precise boundaries. However, the more we attempt to define these boundaries the more arbitrary, unmanageable and ridiculous the machine intelligence becomes.

People think in fuzzy sets but still know what is meant. Red is not a precise definition. It is a set of redness with fuzzy boundaries which change depending on circumstances. Warm is a fuzzy set of temperatures that change according to conditions. True human intelligence requires us to let go of precision and embrace a more flexible way of thinking.

Intelligent machines that are now being manufactured for the market contain chips programmed with fuzzy logic. A heating appliance, sensing that the room temperature has fallen, will not just switch itself on at full blast to restore the preset temperature. It will recognize that the temperature has moved into the fuzzy zone between warm and cold and switch itself half on.

This is a simple example, but the application of fuzzy logic can simplify complex situations, where precise definitions would multiply the 'if this, then that' but 'when that, change this' options into millions. As so often with other technologies, fuzzy logic is just beginning, but in a very few years it will be in all our lives and all our homes. Change the paradigm and the problem becomes solvable.

This is not yet intelligence in the way we humans would recognize intelligence but it is getting closer. There is no reason why these learning systems will not learn how to manoeuvre around furniture in a room whilst doing the cleaning. They will learn how to perform simple medical examinations and operations. They could learn what school subjects a child is finding difficult and reorganize the subject matter to make it more understandable for that child. Ultimately they could remember what are the subjects of conversation you like to talk about and engage you in suitable dialogues. This is the Turing definition of computer intelligence. I personally have no doubt that before the next century is through we will have created computers that will be as intelligent as humans. What I am not sure about is whether we have the ability to create computers that are more intelligent than humans. It sounds as if to do so might turn out to be a contradiction in terms. We may have to use computers to create superhuman intelligence. At this point we will have created a new independent intelligence.

The first early prototype for this type of computer has been built by Professor Igor Aleksander of Imperial College, London. It has been named

Magnus. The Japanese are already into this area of development. In the next century the Japanese will be short of people to do the difficult, dangerous or dirty jobs. These can range from street cleaning to sewer maintenance or entering contaminated areas in nuclear power stations. It could also include boring work such as housework. The Japanese have named these prototypes 'social robots'. The way the western world is introducing the new technology will probably result in there being a surplus of people desperate for these types of jobs.

Education

So far, computing technology has not had as much impact on education as on other areas of life. Schools have not yet downsized on the back of this new technology in the same way that industry and commerce have. Factories of more than 200 or 300 people are increasingly rare but schools of 500 or 1,000 pupils are still common. Why should this be so? The answer is that children have traditionally gone to school because that is where the teachers and the books are to be found. However, with the advent of the super highway, the teachers and the books will be found in the home, courtesy of virtual reality and interactive CD ROMs.

The way children have traditionally been taught has been governed by the technology available to the teachers of the day. For most of the time that has meant that teaching has been carried out with little or no help from technology, relying mainly on blackboard and chalk. It has relied on the skill of the teachers in the way that they have been able to bring the lessons to life and stimulate the imaginations of the children in their care. We have all experienced the effect of inspirational teachers, and we probably did better than average in the subjects that they taught us. Children who have good teachers are lucky. Children who have bad teachers are unlucky, and we have all experienced those too. There is nothing more dull to children than having to sit in ordered rows learning by listening to a bored teacher talking in a bored voice about a subject they see no relevance in, especially when the weather outside is sunny and warm. It is easy to blame the teachers in these circumstances, but it is as well to remember that it is very difficult to put on a sparkling performance for the children time after time. The best stage actors have the greatest difficulty in keeping their enthusiasm going doing repeat performances of long-running shows. How much more difficult it must be for a teacher when the show goes on for year after year and the audience can misbehave.

Yet after school those same children will go home and watch television or play on a computer for hours. If they are lucky they may even have access to the emerging technology of virtual reality. There is something about the visual and the interactive that brings everything alive and grabs the attention, especially of adventurous young children. We absorb more information more quickly in this way than we ever do at school. In fact the average person remembers just 10 per cent of what they read, 20 per cent of what they hear, 30 per cent of what they see, but 90 per cent of what they do. Little wonder that children have preferred to get most of their information from watching television. Little wonder that interactive computer games are now more popular than television, and in the future virtual reality will replace all of these. With virtual reality you don't just experience the scene, you become a part of it.

The technology that has been available to teaching has been reading and writing in books and on blackboards, backed up by explanations from teachers of varying skills. This way of transmitting information from one generation to another has always favoured those children who have been able to absorb information given out in this manner. It has also favoured children of higher natural intelligence who would succeed anyway, whatever the conditions. These two groups make up only a minority of the population. The majority of people are of a more practical turn of mind, and they cannot be catered for by this form of teaching. Consequently it has given rise to an elitist academic concept of education. In the British system until recently, and it is a system that is by no means unique, the exams set for sixteen-year-old children were designed to be passed by the top 40 per cent of the school population. The pass mark was not about who passed but about who got into that top category. They were competitive examinations. The next set of public exams, which act as entry qualifications for university places, were designed to be passed by only 5 per cent of the population. They were competitive to cut down the number of students to the number of places available.

This system, its teaching methods and the technology available to the system, are incapable of passing on information effectively to the majority of the population. The majority of children were, and often still are, expected to accept second best, and further their education at a practical level in work-based apprenticeships. In this respect the British academic educational system may be more extreme than that of other nations but it is in no way unique. All over the world there is a respect attached to being academically gifted, even when some of these people could not survive or find employment outside the ivory towers of academia. What virtual reality is going to do is to bring to every child a teaching method that they can interact with and learn from easily. There will still be a natural gap between those of higher or lower intelligence. There will no longer be a gap between those who can learn from reading and writing, and those who need to experience things to learn them. The majority of the population will now be able to be educated to standards far higher than anything that could be hoped for before.

Virtual reality is still a little clumsy but it is getting smarter by the month. In this area of computer development the technology is moving fast. It is also getting cheaper. The first systems (for games) are expected to hit the market during 1996 at approximately £500 per set. That is cheaper than employing teachers. A class room of thirty desks could be equipped for £15,000 and the equipment would last for five years. That is an annualized cost of £3,000 per year. But why equip a school when the same technology is available in the home? Presented to the hard-headed accountants in the Treasury, a proposal like this has a tendency to seem like an inevitability.

The lessons presented to the children will not be by bored staff fighting to do their best with chalk and blackboard. The lessons will be interactive lessons, personally tailored to each child's speed of learning, and the teachers will be recordings of the most inspirational and memorable teachers that the profession has to offer. Virtual reality will allow each child to experience their lessons in ways even the most fortunate children have not been able to enjoy. Imagine teaching children about music when they can enter a virtual world and conduct an orchestra. Imagine trying to teach children music when they have this facility at home or in amusement arcades but not at school. Government statistics tell us that we have too few children electing to take science courses, possibly because they are perceived as being hard academically. This is probably an accurate perception because the concepts involved in science are so often abstract and outside normal experience. Bad teachers simply add to the confusion in a child's mind. Even trained scientists struggle sometimes, but now they are able to use virtual reality to make their lives easier. For example, the software and hardware already exists that allows complex molecules to appear as larger than life virtual models, right in front of the scientist's eyes. They can walk into these objects and look around them from different angles and they can imagine how one molecule might be slotted into another molecule to make a new compound.

This software technology is still expensive, but it is worth it to the companies who buy it because it can cut months or years off the development time of a commercial project. If it can help trained scientists understand things more easily, just imagine how much more help it will be to children in their education. Just imagine what history lessons would be like if, instead of reading it from a dull book of dates, it could be seen and experienced just as if you were actually there. This was the stuff of science fiction only a few years ago. It is now a cast-iron certainty. If Britain or the West does not invest in this educational technology as it becomes available, and other areas of the world do, then within one generation we will fall behind the best educated people on the planet. The technology has the potential to be that powerful.

Education has favoured the academically minded child and the child who could get along with the traditional methods of teaching. Measured in terms of formal, educational standards, no more than 20 per cent of the school population have had the benefit of leaving school-based, formal education with any form of certified educational standards. New technology will change all that and bring learning and a hunger for knowledge to the majority of children who so far have been left out. If we invest wisely we can look forward to educational standards rising in the future. With technology as powerful as this we must also be careful that other standards do not fall.

The new technology could alter completely the nature of the teaching profession. Using the new technology of virtual reality, children will learn alone, quite possibly at home, and miss out on the acquisition of social skills of mixing and getting on with other people. Teachers would no longer be needed to explain the laws of physics or to help children wrestle with abstract mathematical concepts. They could instead spend their time helping their pupils to develop on a personal basis, and to understand what is involved in being a responsible citizen, tasks that they do not have time for today. In other words, schools could become places where social responsibility is taught and teachers would become personal trainers. Education, like other knowledge-based activities, is destined to become decentralized.

There is something else important to consider in creating a better-educated population, and this has been recognized in a perverse way throughout history. If you educate people you open up their minds to the possibilities of life and also as importantly to its injustices. At the height of the slave trade in the Americas it was a crime, punishable by death in some places, to teach a slave to read or write, in case he got ideas about the injustice he was suffering and rose up against his master. In England in the nineteenth century certain aristocrats, from their positions of privilege in the House of Lords, spoke out against the provision of state primary education, because the lower orders of society would get ideas above their station. The noble lords were afraid that there would be a shortage of people willing to become servants at low wages if education allowed them other options. Both the slavers and the noble lords were right and the ordinary people rebelled against their poverty and exploitation.

If we use technology to provide a better-educated population for the future then society will also have to be prepared to supply a better future. Certainly better-educated individuals will stand a better chance of winning a job for themselves. However, if the early examination system was competitive and designed to exclude all but the most academically gifted from the few places available, what will the reaction of a better-educated population be if a substantial majority are competitively excluded from the work available? If there are just not enough jobs to go round then those who are left out will know that, even having the ability, they have been badly treated. If society does not cater for them, then substantial numbers of disillusioned young people will come to regard society as their enemy and not their friend. Subcultures are already developing amongst the 20 per cent of the population who today live in poverty. When reinforced by feelings of religious oppression, as in Northern Ireland, the Lebanon or Bosnia, they can easily turn violent. In America there are whole districts of economically underprivileged people that can turn violent when provoked. The case of Rodney King in Los Angeles is the most recent example. New housing developments for middle-class families are often built within perimeter walls with armed security guards at the gated entrances. It is already estimated that 4,000,000 Americans live in these types of segregated communities. The Third World is reappearing in the heart of the First World. Is this any way to live or organize society?

Medicine

Computer technology is not the only frontier that science is pushing back. Medical knowledge is making rapid progress as well. We are all going to live longer and be healthier. The average lifespan in Shakespeare's time was under forty years of age. It wasn't much better in the last century. A lot of people did live to be sixty or seventy years of age but even more people died as infants. Since the nineteenth century most of the medical advances that have been made that have increased people's lifespans have been in the area of reducing infant mortality. This is what has pushed up the figures that show that on average people are living longer. The sums work in this way. When working out averages the inclusion of zero figures drags the result down dramatically. Ten people living to the age of seventy and ten children dying at birth give an average life expectancy of thirty-five years for the group. Nineteen people living until they are seventy and one person dying at birth gives a life expectancy of sixty-six years for the group. This is also the profile of a population in which most of the people are of working age, i.e. twenty to sixty years of age. The young are the most significant group of dependants. Medical science has rightly concentrated on the task of saving young lives, and with spectacular results. Very few children now die at birth or in infancy.

In the Western world the average lifespan is now over seventy years and is slowly rising. Significant numbers of people are living into their eighties and increasingly into their nineties. This is due to medical science turning its resources away from the battle against infant mortality, which it has won, and concentrating them on the attack against disease. Each year we learn how to prevent, cure or postpone the onset of ever more illnesses that would prove fatal if they ran their natural course. Very few people die of old age; they die of cancer or a heart attack or some other illness. The more we conquer these illnesses the longer people will live in a real sense and not just as an arithmetic average. Thus it is unavoidable that the number of dependants in the population will rise and need supporting by those of working age. The population profile will change fundamentally.

Doctors and scientists are now studying seriously the subject of ageing, and asking the question 'Why does it happen?' The longest male life recorded is that of Shigechiyo Isumi of Japan who lived 120 years and 207 days. If one person can do it why can't everyone? What did Shigechiyo have in his genes that enabled him to live so long? Could this secret be discovered, replicated and transferred to others to enable them to live as long or even longer? This is the secret of life that the human race has been seeking ever since man first became conscious of the inevitability of death. This secret is worth more than almost anything that science will ever discover. Spurred on by the prospect of being able to patent the knowledge and make countless billions of pounds out of its exploitation, this is now the starting point of a world-wide race between scientists to sequence human DNA and RNA, and thereby discover exactly how our genes control our lives and deaths. There are more than 350 laboratories world-wide working on the project, with a total investment of over \$3 billion. The final sequencing of the human genetic code was scheduled to be completed by the year 2005. However in September 1994 researchers at the Argonne National Laboratory near Chicago, funded by the US Department of Energy, announced that they had developed a superfast computer chip to speed up the process. Hyseq Inc of California were reported as holding the patent rights on the chip, and now predict the completion of the process by 1997. Already, by September 1995, 40 per cent of the work had been done.

There might be a gene in there that could be switched off so the clock of ageing stops running. It could be that there is no clock, but that the genes that control the repair and renewal functions in the body switch off, or give up progressively after we pass beyond the age of being fertile, and that they could be switched back on. The latest theory that I heard suggests that the DNA chain is like a piece of shoe lace which gets frayed at the ends as time passes. The useful pieces of DNA are interspersed with many more non-essential pieces of DNA. So long as the fraying only affects the non-essentials then nothing much goes wrong, but when it destroys an essential piece the cell dies or turns cancerous. There is a protein that acts in the same way as the piece of plastic at the end of shoe laces to prevent them from fraying. It is abundant in young cells but is missing in older cells. Ways are being sought to prevent its loss from the older cells and so extend their lifespan. We don't yet know, but we will know very soon. Certainly we will know within the next ten, or at most twenty, years and, like the nuclear bomb, once the technology is discovered the knowledge cannot be undiscovered. This knowledge is costing money to discover so it will be exploited to recover the investment and more. How we will adjust to it will be one of the most momentous moral debates of all time. It will be impossible to reserve it for some and deny it to others. It will be worth doing anything to get the treatment, even killing, because without it you would die anyway. If we all did become everlasting in the sense of not dying through biological malfunction, then there would still be death by accidental causes. This would limit the average lifespan to between 100,000 and 200,000 years. This is science fiction territory, but so were nuclear weapons before 1945.

The issue is that of how we are going to deal with an ageing population. Is the retirement age going to be pushed up to eighty or ninety years of age? Is the workforce going to be swelled by millions of extra workers unable to compete with the younger generations for the diminishing number of jobs available? Most people struggle hard to save enough pension money to see them through to their mid seventies. Imagine the amount of money you would have to save over a working life of forty years if that money had to support you for a further forty years after retirement at the same standard of living. On the assumption that the effects of compound interest will be cancelled out by the effects of inflation, then preparation for forty years of retirement will entail the saving of between twenty-five and fifty per cent of salary from the first day of work, depending on the rates of interest prevailing when the final annuity is purchased. This is an impossibility. It is impossible on a personal level and it is revolutionary on a social level. Savings at these rates would radically alter today's economy, initially stripping out vast swathes of consumer spending, lowering living standards and devastating the job creation prospects of whole sectors of the economy. In the longer term only a fully automated and robotized economy will be able to support these levels of dependency as people regularly live longer in retirement than they spend in work.

Once again, astute politicians, realizing the enormity of the problem if tackled from the traditional mindset of economics that they are trapped within, are busy solving the issue by side-stepping it. 'In the future', they declare, 'people will have the freedom to make their own pension arrangements to suit themselves'. Some people certainly can, but the majority have not a hope in hell of providing for old age.

A survey commissioned by the *Observer* newspaper[2] in conjunction with a respected firm of actuaries has shown that in order to generate a pension equivalent to two thirds of final salary at a retirement age of sixty-five, a person will have to save and invest 15 per cent of annual salary every year from the age of twenty-seven, a period of thirty-eight years. However, if you are out of work or low-paid, 15 per cent is just not available to be saved, and a pension of two thirds of a poverty wage is just deeper poverty anyway.

The pensioners who do best are those in schemes where the employer contributes to and guarantees a pension of two thirds final salary, but there is a problem here too. These schemes are based on the concept of forty years' employment with one employer. Anyone who changes jobs breaks the assumptions on which the calculations are based. An executive changing jobs every ten years can expect to accumulate assorted pension benefits of only 39 per cent of final salary. But is not this flexibility the working pattern of the future that we are all expected to buy into? Even the UK state pension is not safe. As the tax base of the economy of those in full-time work continues to decline, so the state pension is being manipulated to decline also, by fixing it to the retail price index instead of relating it to average earnings. A lot of old people are going to be very poor in the future and they have every right to be angry about it.

This may prove to be the catalyst for change. Governments can side-step the issue by pulling out of the provision of pensions and pushing the responsibility back on to individuals and private pension arrangements. Private pension schemes can do what they can and then withdraw, when they have returned the pension entitlements to the policyholders to the limit of the provisions contracted for. Society, however, cannot avoid the prospect of tens of thousands, if not millions, of old people in need of care but with no money to pay for it. We can avoid our responsibility to children by blaming the parents for not providing the necessary care. We can avoid our responsibility towards unemployed people by branding them as lazy. We cannot make any such excuses about our failure towards old people. They have worked in their lifetimes as required and paid what they can towards their pension arrangements. They are past working age and cannot be expected to rejoin the labour force. They have no means of earning money. They simply have to have the care and physical necessities that they require. There is no valid reason why they should not have everything they need. The system can produce enough to service all their requirements. There are food stores all over Europe and North America that contain tens of thousands of tons of surplus food. There is enough electrical generating capacity to heat pensioners' houses to healthy temperatures several times over. However, pensioners are hungry and pensioners are cold, and they live in reduced circumstances because they are trying to survive on totally inadequate state and private pensions. It is an absolute nonsense. They can't afford what they need and we say that we can't afford to give them what they need. Yet the system has the ability to produce what they need, and the surpluses of food, energy, and everything else are looking us right in the face. The pensioners do have one thing on their side, and that is the vote. As their numbers increase they will become the most important voting block in the electorate. They can and should simply vote themselves what they need and ignore the cost. The cost is a false, self-imposed restriction on the system's ability to deliver. The politicians will find a way around the problem when they are made to, when they free their minds from the idea that everything still has to be paid for, even though the economy is running on automatic.

Biotechnology

Developments in biotechnology share much in common with developments in the medical sciences. They are both extending our knowledge of biological systems. The twentieth century is sometimes referred to as the century of physics. The twenty-first century could turn out to be the century of biology. Physics has been applied to understanding the building blocks of atoms so that we can recombine them by the application of energy or decombine them for the release of energy. Biotechnology is about understanding how molecules can be made to work together, and combine and recombine naturally so that we can grow things into existence.

Until now, human beings have had to wrest what they want from nature. To make an iron implement requires that the iron ore be dug from the ground. It then has to be heated to great temperatures, possibly by burning coal which also has to be won from deep within the earth. The resulting metal then has to be fashioned into shape and drilled, cut, polished, and more until a finished product emerges. It is a process that involves energy and waste. It involves forcing materials together into unwilling combinations. Nature does not work in this way.

A tiny seed contains a set of instructions that tells the molecules what they must do in order to create a mighty oak tree or a human being. From two cells, male and female, millions of molecules are arranged to make the most complex and intelligent of structures on the earth, ourselves. The instructions read something like the instructions that follow.

'First find some more molecules with which you can work, then arrange them as copies of yourself and tell them to do the same. After a given number of times reproducing copies of yourselves, stop doing so. Next, half of you are going to become the right side and half are going to become the left side. Find some more molecules to work with and continue arranging yourselves in this new way until it is time for another change of direction.'

Just like the wizard of old waving the magic wand and commanding the molecules of the elements to rise up in the form of his choosing, we are close to understanding how the trick is done. We already know that it is accomplished without the wasteful application of resources to force the elements together. Living things are not fashioned in the heat of furnaces. At the molecular level the atoms are assembled using a toolset that we are just beginning to understand. All the process needs is a supply of willing molecules and a friendly, nourishing environment.

It is an incredibly efficient manufacturing system. All you have to do is hand down the right set of instructions in the form of a tiny seed or a string of DNA and leave well alone. When we finally read these instructions they will show us a way of doing things that will be beautiful in its simplicity and awesome in its power. Used properly, the products of this next scientific revolution will change and enrich our lives more than all the brute force technology of the Industrial Revolution. All you have to do is to use your imagination to see what can be achieved. For example, a tree is a solar-powered water pump. From its roots deep in the soil it transports water up to its highest branches and leaves. In the largest trees this can be a lift of over 100 metres. It would take a large mechanical pump to achieve this same result.

Today's food crops will be genetically engineered and made disease-resistant and frost-hardy. Tropical fruits will then be able to thrive right up to the Polar circles. New crops that are in themselves complete foods and which could be eaten straight from the plant will be developed each with its own attractive flavour. Today's soya bean, more commonly recognized as the baked bean, is a protein source only one amino acid short of the complete range of amino acids people need to sustain health. Human adults need nine amino acids from which to fashion the proteins of bone, muscle, tendon and skin that constitute the human body. The soya plant contains eight of them. Other plants are rich in carbohydrates, oils, vitamins and minerals. Rearranging plant RNA and DNA to make complete food varieties is not a dream. Nor is the possibility of making these new plants self-seeding so that all a person would have to do to enjoy a meal would be to walk along a country path and pick whatever took their fancy and eat it there and then. Our prehistoric ancestors had to find their food where they could, and nature was not always kind. Today we grow food in one part of the world, trade in it, ship it hundreds or thousands of miles, process it into an edible form and deliver it to shops from where customers collect it. The original cash value of the nutritional content ends up as a small part of the total price. It is not an efficient system compared with what could eventually be available on everyone's doorstep and possibly for free. The legal precedent is already established. If you enter on to land and pick a crop that a farmer has sown and cultivated then that is stealing. However, if you enter on to land and pick a crop that nature has sown then that is free and always has been. Fruit in the hedgerows and mushrooms in the pastures are, in the UK, legally free food there for the taking today. In the future it might be possible to pick up the equivalent of a three-course meal from the same source.

This green revolution will not be able to replace all the mechanical devices our knowledge has created so far, but it has more potential than many people realize. In the formation of bone and wood we have two materials that possess considerable and long-lasting structural and load-bearing properties. Electric eels generate and store considerable charges of electricity. Certain microbes positively enjoy eating molecules of metal and concentrating them in their tiny bodies. Rubber is from plants. Oil is the organic remains of prehistoric creatures. What we have nearly described are the materials it takes to make a motor car! However any motor vehicle 'grown' through the application of green technology will be as different from today's grand prix racer as that is in turn from the first horse-drawn chariot!

Biotechnology is finding its way into all sorts of new areas. It is being used to fashion new medicines. It is being used to alter the genetic structures of animals to make them more useful to human beings in, for example, the production of medicines. It is possible that inherited diseases such as cystic fibrosis could be eliminated by genetically altering the embryo before it starts growing in the womb. The possibilities are endless, and in the next 100 years this science will turn our world upside down. What we must remember is that even if we can't see the precise nature of the developments now, they will still happen. Human knowledge is doubling every ten years and that guarantees that there will be change.

Biotechnology is about letting nature do the work. It is about creating things by handing down a set of genetic instructions and letting nature get on with the job. In the industrial age, manufacturing was about handing down a set of instructions and expecting a human workforce to do the job. Biotechnology is going to create jobs for scientists and technicians during its development phase but as soon as that is over it will have little need for human workers.

Physics

Physics still has many promises it yet has to fulfil. In the 1930s splitting the atom was the holy grail of this science. Nuclear fission involves starting a chain reaction in which the heaviest atoms, such as uranium, are encouraged to split down into lighter and more stable elements, and in the process give up some of their energy in the form of heat. Handled incorrectly or in the wrong hands, the release of energy is not a steady process but an uncontrolled nuclear explosion. The by-products of either process contain some substances that are powerful and deadly poisons to most life forms on earth. Nuclear fission was the first attack on the power of the atom because it is the easiest.

Nuclear fusion is the opposite of fission. It involves forcing molecules of the lightest elements to join together and in the process give up some of their energy in the form of heat. It is the process that is going on in the sun and is the energy source that allows life to exist on earth. The by-product that results from forcing two atoms of hydrogen together is the harmless gas helium. There is enough free hydrogen in the world's oceans to last for millions of years and it is there for the taking. In order to force the hydrogen atoms together it is necessary to replicate the intense temperatures of the sun in a confined way here on earth. Scientists have already done this for a few seconds but the work still has a long way to go. The latest achievement in the world-wide race to exploit this nearly free energy source is a conversion ratio of four to one. In other words, it took four units of energy in to create one unit of energy out. The gap is getting narrower. Few doubt that eventually it will be successful. When the breakthrough comes it will be time to sell shares in electricity companies, because the cost of generating electric power will fall through the floor.

There was a possible false lead in the race to find fusion when Professors Fleischmann and Ponds announced that they had discovered 'cold fusion'. If true, this method would remove the need to generate the extraordinarily high temperatures that are holding up the progress of 'hot fusion' research. This whole subject is surrounded by controversy, but it is worth remembering that the major scientific breakthroughs came from people who dared think the unthinkable and forced a paradigm shift onto the world. Thereafter it is the role of the more conventionally inclined to take the new knowledge and systematically exploit its potential.

The race is also on to discover materials that superconduct electricity at room temperatures. Most materials superconduct at temperatures approaching absolute zero (minus 273 degrees Celsius) but some have been discovered that superconduct at much higher temperatures. Why this should be so is not yet fully understood, but when substances can be found that superconduct at room temperature then it will be possible to transmit electricity over any distance without loss of power on the way. Cheap electricity and cheap power transmission will revolutionize the provision of energy in the next century.

Conclusion

The developments described above are not going to affect our lives too much during the remaining few years of this century. It is quite normal for new ideas to take twenty or thirty years to come through to the market place after they have been proved feasible in the laboratory. Life-saving air bags were advertized in the *National Geographic* magazine in 1972 but are only now being fitted to cars over twenty years later. Some of the developments described are still awaiting other scientific developments to complete the chain of technology, and the timescales for those developments are unpredictable. However, there is little doubt that they will occur in one form or another. Short-term profit takers can ignore them but medium-term planners ignore them at their peril.

The advances in computer science will be available first because they are nearing the deliverable stage already. We are now used to the impact of computerization in the commercial world but we are unprepared for its impact in the world of education. The medical advances will also happen reasonably quickly. People will demand them once it is generally appreciated that they can extend the quality and length of life. By the year 2020 both the extended use of computers and the extension of human life will be commonplace. It will take longer for biological engineering to impact, because although the technology is becoming commonplace there is regulator concern over the impact of such changes on the environment. The physics of fusion still awaits the necessary scientific breakthrough. However, children born today will experience it all in their lifetimes.

These advances can be seen as problems that will overwhelm us or as opportunities to be grasped with both hands. On the one hand computerization will continue to destroy existing jobs. Medical advances will continue to increase the number of dependants that society will have to support. Biotechnology will change the way our economy works and in the process disrupt the existing order of things. In the future there will be too few jobs, as we understand the word today, to support through taxation the number of dependants that will make up the vast majority of society. On the other hand computerized machines will have the potential to deliver the goods and services that we all need, and nuclear fusion will deliver free electricity. In these circumstances society will either change or drive itself into the ground. The next generations will be either the richest or the most divided in our brief history.

The problem is simply this. For most of their history human beings have had to compete with the natural elements for the means to survive. Nature is 'red in tooth and claw' and it is entirely to be expected that, over centuries, human attitudes have been shaped by this dictum. Humans have had to compete to survive and have learnt to be as hard towards each other as they have had to be towards nature in the battle for food and shelter. This has given rise to the underlying morals and attitudes of our economic system. These are that people can only consume that which they own, and if they do not own anything they can only consume that for which they work. Money today is the token that shows that a person has fulfilled one or both of these criteria.

These are necessary and sensible rules in a world of shortages. They are entirely inappropriate in a world of plenty, and the future has the potential to be a world of plenty. Indeed these principles are so deeply ingrained that if we are surprised by a surplus we will destroy it and stand down the means of production, rather than see it handed out for free. We can see the start of this process today. Agricultural land is removed from production even though there are hungry people. Building workers are unemployed even though there are homeless people. There are waiting lists for hospital treatment even though there are doctors and nurses enough to deliver the medical treatment. There are old people going without the basic necessities of life even though the means to provide for their needs exist in plenty all around them. The system is enforcing a moral judgement that is being made redundant by technology. The system sees money as the proof that a person has played a part in creating the goods and services available and is therefore entitled to consume them. There was a time when not working meant that a person was a burden on his fellow citizens and not entitled to any surplus they might have created unless it was given through acts of charity. In the future not working will mean that a person is only a burden on the machines that took away the need for him to work in the first place.

People are the most expensive way of making things and technology is the cheapest way. It makes absolute sense, using current economic criteria, to replace people with technology. As technology gets cheaper and people want to get richer, it is inevitable that people will be replaced by machines just as soon as the technology allows.

A specific example of new computer technology was quoted above. There now exists computer software that will listen to the human voice and translate the words spoken directly into print. Hundreds of thousands of typists and secretaries make their living by doing this job today. This is not fiction; the product can be purchased now. The average secretary costs an employer somewhere in the region of £15–20,000 a year. This voice recognition software package cost approximately £4,000 twelve months ago and its price has fallen to around £1,000 at the time of writing. There is no economic argument for not using it. Once word gets out, every company will be using it. If there is a bright spot in the unemployment figures it is that employment for women has been rising and compensating for some of the decline in number of jobs available to men. The impact that this software will have on the trend can only be guessed at.

People are right to see a threat to their standards of living in the new science and technology, if the advances are blindly and single-mindedly applied to reducing costs with no regard for their wider implications. In the past, frightened workers have tried to stop the introduction of new methods by smashing the machines that were taking away their jobs. They became known as Luddites after their leader. There is no future in being a modern Luddite and trying to stop the advance of science and technology. There is a brilliant future awaiting, if we can work out how it can be managed so that it benefits everyone and liberates us all from so much of the soul-destroying work we have to do today.

Notes

Chapter 1   Are We on a Fool's Journey?

1   Andre Gorz, *Capitalism, Socialism, Ecology*, tr. Chris Turner (Verso, 1994), p. 22.
2   John Kavanagh, 'News and Views About Jobs', *Computer Weekly*, 29 Sep. 1994.
3   Tony Jackson, Martin Dickson and Louise Kehoe, 'Once more unto the Breach', *Financial Times*, 7 Feb. 1994.
4   John B. Judis, 'What's the Deal', *Mother Jones*, March/April 1994.
5   David Halberstram, *The Next Century* (Avon Books, New York, 1992), p. 75.
6   Kevin Philips, *The Politics of Rich and Poor* (Harper Perennial, New York, 1991), p. 17.
7   *For Richer, For Poorer; the Changing Distribution of Income in the UK 1961–1991* (Institute for Fiscal Studies, 7 Ridgemount Street, London, WC1E 7RA).
8   Interview, BBC Radio 4, 23 Sep. 1995.

Chapter 2   Looking the Gift Horse in the Mouth

1   World Industrial Robots 1994. Ref GVE 94.0.24. UN Sales Section, Palais Des Nations, CH – 1211, Geneva 10.

Chapter 4   Progress is Three Per Cent

1   *Times Top 1000*, Harper Collins.
2   Mike Cassell and Gillian Tett, 'Feel the quality, not the width', *Financial Times*, 29 Aug. 1994.
3   *Outlook 55*, OECD.

Chapter 5 Can Everything be Saved?

1 Figures computed from *The Economist* 'Pocket Britain in Figures' (Hamish Hamilton, 1995).
2 *Computer Business Review*, vol. 3, no. 1, January 1995, ISSN 1350–4665.

Chapter 6 Which Jobs will Grow and Which Jobs will Go?

1 The Economist 'Pocket Britain in Figures' (Hamish Hamilton, 1995).
2 Martin O'Halloran, *Sunday Mirror*, 10 Sep. 1995.
3 Norman Macrae, 'Has the middle class had its chips?', *Sunday Times*, 4 Dec. 1994.
4 *Management Today*, Feb. 1995.
5 'Is a superfluous population becoming an American fixture?', *Barron's*, Sep. 1994.
6 Frank Swoboda, *The Washington Post*, 24 Sep. 1994.
7 Peter Drucker, 'Managing the social sector', *The Washington Times*, 3 Nov. 1994.
8 'The New World of Work', *Business Week*, 7 Oct. 1994.
9 Charles Handy, *The Future of Work* (Blackwell, Oxford, 1985), p. 155.
10 *Calgary Sun*, 7 Aug. 1995.

Chapter 7 Can We Rely on the Enterprise Culture and the Small Business to Solve our Problems?

1 Central Statistical Office, *Size Analysis of United Kingdom Businesses 1993*.
2 *The Economist* 'Pocket Britain in Figures' (Hamish Hamilton, 1995).
3 Geoffrey A. Moore, *Crossing the Chasm* (Harper Business, New York, 1996).

Chapter 8 Capitalism Channelled by Technology

1 Jeremy Rifkin, *The End Of Work* (G.P. Putman and Sons, New York, 1995), pp. 25–29.
2 Paul Krugman, *Peddling Prosperity* (W.W. Norton & Company, New York, 1995), p. 46.
3 Julian Beltrame, 'In the US, the question is asked: Whose economy is it?', *Vancouver Sun*, 8 Aug. 1995.
4 David Smith, 'Economic Outlook', *Sunday Times*, 24 Sep. 1995.
5 Eli Berman, John Bound, Zri Griliches, 'Changes in the demand for skilled labor within US manufacturing industries', Working Paper 4255, NBER, 1050 Mass Ave, Cambridge, MA 02138. Quoted by Edward Balls in 'Developed country victims of the technological age', *Financial Times*, March 1993.
6 David Evans, *Computer Weekly*, 22 Sep. 1994.

7   The Institute of Management, 2 Savoy Court, Strand, London, WC2R OEZ in conjunction with Manpower plc., August 1994.

Chapter 10   Do Other Cultures Behave Differently?

1   *The Economist* 'Pocket World in Figures' (Penguin Group, London, 1995).
2   Charles Hampden-Turner and Fons Trompenaars, *The Seven Cultures of Capitalism* (Doubleday, New York, 1993), p. 60.
3   A fuller description of the subject is found in Jonathan Charkham, *Keeping Good Company – A study of corporate governance in five countries* (Clarendon Press, Oxford, 1994).
4   *The Seven Cultures of Capitalism*, p. 167.
5   Michel Albert, *Capitalism Against Capitalism* (Whurr Publishers Ltd, London, 1993).
6   Gary Katzenstein, *Funny Business – An Outsider's Year in Japan* (Grafton Books, London, 1990).
7   Bureau of Labour Statistics, *Employment & Earnings*, March 1994.
8   European Commission, *Employment in Europe 1994.*
9   *The Seven Cultures of Capitalism*, p. 165.

Chapter 11   Multinational Companies, Global Companies and International Trade

1   *The Economist* 'Pocket World in Figures' (Penguin Group, London, 1995), pp. 22, 53.
2   'Multinationals Face Tax Attack', *Sunday Times*, 9 Oct. 1994.
3   Matthew Horsman and Jeremy Warner, 'Revealed: Murdoch's Tax Holiday', *Independent*, 27 Nov. 1995.
4   Nicholas R. Lardy, *China in the World Economy* (Washington D.C. Institute for International Economics, April 1994).
5   Chinese Academy of Social Sciences, *Policy Choices of China's Economic Development.*
6   *World Competitiveness Report* (1994), IMD, CH-1007 Lausanne.
7   'Labour costs force group(s) to join trend in switching production to Asia and Eastern Europe', *Financial Times*, 12 Sep. 1995.
8   Ross Perot, *Not for Sale at Any Price* (Hyperion, New York, 1993), p. 137.

Chapter 12   The Weird and Wonderful World of International Finance

1   Kenichi Ohmae, *The Borderless World* (Harper Business, New York, 1990), p. 160.
2   Joel Kurtzman, *The Death of Money* (Simon & Schuster, New York, 1993).
3   Richard Thomson, 'City Grasps Lion's Share', *Independent*, 4 Sep. 1994.

4   Tracy Corrigan, 'On Trial for Dangerous Dealing', *Financial Times*, 21 March 1994.
5   John Plender, 'Through a Market Darkly', *Financial Times*, 1994.
6   John Plender, 'High Wire Act in a Bear Garden', *Financial Times*, 1994.
7   Robert Kutter, 'Blasphemy From Blinder?', *Business Week*, 26 Sep. 1994.

Chapter 13   The Paradigm Shift

1   *Sunday Times*, 30 April 1995.
2   T. S. Kuhn, *Structure of Scientific Revolutions* (Chicago University Press, Il., 1970).
3   Charles Handy, *The Future of Work* (Blackwell, Oxford, 1985), p. 14.

Chapter 14   The Future

1   Department of Trade and Industry, 151 Buckingham Palace Road, London.
2   Neasa MacErlean, 'Bleak new world for pensioners', *Observer*, 17 April 1994.

Index

N.B. Page references to figures and tables are *italicized*